To Br

Problem Hunting

Problem Hunting

The Tech Startup Textbook

BRIAN LONG

Peakpoint Press books may be purchased in bulk at special discounts for sales promotion, corporate gifts, fund-raising, or educational purposes. Special editions can also be created to specifications. For details, contact the Special Sales Department, Skyhorse Publishing, 307 West 36th Street, 11th Floor, New York, NY 10018 or info@skyhorsepublishing.com.

Visit our website at www.skyhorsepublishing.com.

10 9 8 7 6 5 4 3 2 1

Library of Congress Cataloging-in-Publication Data is available on file.

Cover design by David Ter-Avanesyan

ISBN: 978-1-5107-7796-5
Ebook ISBN: 978-1-5107-7866-5

Printed in the United States of America

Dedication

This book is dedicated to my wife, Liz, who has supported me to pursue every crazy business idea over the last eighteen years with brilliance, patience, and love. To our daughter Claudia, who loves to share and has helped inspire me to put something in writing to share with other people. I also wouldn't be here without the incredible support from my parents, Kathleen Long and David Long, who encouraged me to pursue what I loved, and my sisters Katrina and Amy, who pushed me to keep up with their genius and excellence.

Contents

Introduction

In the world of startup business books, I've found great strategy books, countless war stories, and many volumes of management advice—but I've struggled to discover a book that focuses on the practical steps in finding and launching a new tech business.

I've written this book as a tactical textbook to start a tech company, based on my experience starting two successful software companies over the last ten years. The first one, TapCommerce, was only around for two years and sold to Twitter in 2014 for ~$100 million. The second one, Attentive, has grown to ~1,000 employees and hundreds of millions in revenue and raised ~$850 million in venture capital.

Most of my companies have been in software, but this book will help any entrepreneur. This book is broken down into sections covering the critical aspects and departments for starting and scaling a tech company. It is roughly organized in the chronological sequence with which I would start a business today, but is also designed so that you can quickly jump to a section for help or guidance as you need it, so don't feel the need to read it straight through.

I love startup businesses and the entrepreneurs who boldly decide to start them. Startups can solve big problems, create jobs, and develop new generations of entrepreneurs. I hope this book helps you along your startup journey. Now let's get going!

Part 1
Product Market Fit

There is a magical moment in the life of a successful startup company when everything suddenly starts to work. Customers start buying the product like crazy, the industry is beginning to notice your business, and people actually want to talk to you. This is called obtaining "product market fit," and it should be the first goal of a tech startup entrepreneur, because it means your business is working. It is also really hard to achieve.

The chapters in this part will help you to find a burning problem for your business to solve, cheaply test different solutions, and build your first product. My experiences and guidance in this part are skewed toward enterprise software, but most of the concepts can be applied to any startup business.

CHAPTER 1
Problem Hunting

So you want to start a company, but you don't know what the company should do? That's okay. I have talked to thousands of entrepreneurs, and everyone has this issue at some point. I've had it myself. This is the first step in the process.

Building your business starts by finding a truly burning customer problem. Problem hunting is serious work. You will need to spend a lot of time listening to potential buyers, learning about what makes them tick, and gaining their trust to share their biggest problems.

The good news is that the world is full of problems across wide sets of industries and consumers. Better yet, there are new problems being created every day, and there are many solutions that no longer work. There is an incredible amount of opportunity for new business creation to solve real problems.

In this chapter, we will set a process for identifying customer problems. We will start by analyzing different groups of markets, identifying individual buyers within those markets, and then establishing a process for talking to buyers in order to get as much information as possible. It is your job to make sure the problems you have identified are truly important, otherwise your business will struggle to sell its products.

Principles of Problem Hunting

1. **Start with a large growing market.** A rising tide lifts all boats.
2. **Identify buyers.** For consumer-oriented businesses you can break it down to cohorts, and for business-to-business sales you need to find employees with decision-making authority.
3. **Create a list and schedule meetings with buyers.** Use a variety of digital tools to engage your buyers.
4. **Get qualitative and quantitative feedback from interviews.** Listen closely to your buyer, and press to find their biggest problems.
5. **Create and refine a problem definition document (PDD).** Define the critical problems of your buyer. We will use this later to build and test your solutions.
6. **Make sure you like the problem.** You will be more likely to succeed and enjoy your work if you pick an industry you are interested in.

Start with a Large Growing Market

Getting a small piece of a massive market is usually a lot easier than getting a massive piece of a small market. As a result, most successful startup businesses tend to focus on larger markets. An IBISWorld report, "Biggest Industries by Revenue in the US in 2023,"[1] identifies those industries as:

1 Ibisworld.com/united-states/industry-trends/biggest-industries-by-revenue/.

Rank	Industry (in the US)	Revenue for 2023 (In Billions)
1	Hospitals	$1,426
2	Health & Medical Insurance	$1,246
3	Commercial Banking	$1,210
4	Drug, Cosmetic & Toiletry Wholesaling	$1,202
5	New Car Dealers	$1,124
6	Life Insurance & Annuities	$1,121
7	Pharmaceuticals Wholesaling	$1,102
8	Public Schools	$995
9	E-Commerce & Online Auctions	$934
10	Gasoline & Petroleum Wholesaling	$928

You should rerun this analysis for your present day. Do you see any categories that you like? Circle the ones that you like and add them to your list of areas you want to focus on for problem hunting. If you extend this list, you will likely also find massive markets such as supermarkets, colleges, wholesale, real estate, and energy. If you are outside the United States, the list may be a bit different, but it typically comes back to the basics of life: shelter, food, health, transportation, clothing, education, energy, and finance.

It can be easier to grow if your market is also growing really fast, creating massive demand for any new market entrant. You should search for markets that are growing really rapidly. According to IBISWorld, here are the "10 Fastest Growing Industries in the US by Revenue Growth (%) in 2023."[2]

2 Ibisworld.com/united-states/industry-trends/fastest-growing-industries/.

Rank	Industry (in the US)	2023–2024 Revenue Growth
1	CBD Product Manufacturing	28%
2	Solar Power	25.5%
3	International Airlines	24.9%
4	Unmanned Aerial Vehicles (UAV) Manufacturing	24.8%
5	Tour Operators	24.4%
6	Hotels & Motels	22.8%
7	Hybrid & Electric Vehicle Manufacturing	22%
8	Sightseeing Transportation	20.6%
9	Commercial Banking	19.7%
10	Smart Thermostat Manufacturing	19.1%

Do any of these jump off the page to you?

In addition to market size and experience, it is important that you find a market that is interesting to you. Years ago, my cofounders and I started a used clothing marketplace for higher-end fashion. We called it Sell My Closet. We made a mobile phone application, posted some initial listings, and asked people to post their own listings. We got a ton of stuff listed by hundreds of people in our first week, including even bright green underwear. We spent hours looking at clothing listings and talking about fashion, and each day felt incredibly long and tedious. We walked away from the idea because we just couldn't get excited about a marketplace for reselling clothes. Other companies such as Poshmark and thredUP went on to build large businesses helping to recycle clothing. It was a good idea, but it wouldn't have worked for us. Startups require the self-motivation to get up and push each day. We just couldn't get excited about fashion.

Identify Buyers

Now that you have a market you are interested in exploring, you need to talk to your potential customers to explore their problems. So who should you talk to? This depends on the type of business you want to build: a consumer-facing business or a B2B business?

For Consumer Businesses (B2C)

For a consumer business (B2C), where you are selling to individual people rather than businesses, you need to identify your target customer groups, develop a system to engage them, and ask them questions to explore their problems. The good news is that each adult typically has their own decision-making authority. The bad news is that each adult is different, so your challenge is to find the common problems shared across large groups of people.

When I was growing up, I thought soda was not sweet enough. I wanted to create a brand of soda that could be customized to the sweetness level of the drinker. The soda would be purchased with the syrup and the seltzer in separate containers. The consumer could then combine the two liquids to their taste preference, and enjoy the drink. While this product solved my yearning for a tooth-decaying level of sweetness, it was not shared by many fellow consumers. Furthermore, if a consumer did want a sweeter beverage, they didn't want to mix it on their own and deal with spills and sticky hands. I built the product for just me, rather than for a group of consumers. You need to talk to a lot of consumers and find a problem shared across a large group of people.

Consumers are easy to engage in two simple steps: create an online form and drive traffic to that form. For some of our early experiments in Attentive, we wanted to talk to the consumers to understand why they would sign up to receive text messages from businesses. To reach these consumers, we created a quick survey using Google Forms. Google Forms is free and quite robust; you can set it up in just a few minutes. Our survey collected name, email, phone number, and a few questions relevant to our problem, such as, "What type of text messages do you want to receive from businesses?" We also included a question asking if the consumer would be open to a follow-up phone call with our team for $50, which allowed us to conduct longer follow-up conversations. If you are looking for more advanced survey features, you might also look into SurveyMonkey by Momentive, Qualtrics, or Typeform.

Now that you have a landing page to collect feedback, you need to drive consumers to the page. Not all web traffic is created equal. Some forms of traffic will be cheap or free but might drive consumers who don't match your target audience. For instance, you can post your survey for free on Craigslist or a social media feed, but that could drive respondents from almost anywhere.

For a more targeted approach, make a copy of your sign-up form just for paid advertising. Now go to Google Ads and Meta Ads and set up a small advertising campaign to drive traffic to your landing page. On these platforms, you can target specific cohorts of customers to help ensure you are reaching the type of consumers you want to sell your product to. Using these strategies, we were able to get thousands of consumer survey responses, and conduct dozens of detailed in-person focus group discussions. These discussions will be invaluable in helping you to identify the consumer problem you want to solve.

For Business to Business (B2B)

For a business-to-business venture (B2B), where you are selling your product to other businesses, you need to find the people that have the authority to purchase things on behalf of their company.

In my company Franklin, our product was a tool for big distributed workforces to communicate via text message. Using our software, executives and managers could easily send mass communications to their workforce and also collect responses and feedback via SMS.

We predominantly sold our software to the human resources (HR) department, usually targeting someone with a title like the vice president of human resources. HR was a very nice department, and not particularly busy, so they were always open to taking calls. On the calls, HR was engaged and interested in pitch meetings, and we felt like we were really on to something. We set up hundreds of meetings, got lots of positive feedback, but never sold a dollar.

Unfortunately, HR had no money to pay for our solution. The limited budget they had was deployed rather slowly, and implementation time lines ran over the course of several years. We couldn't wait several years to earn our first dollars. HR was generally viewed as a back-office cost center. As a result, HR had no budget and little prioritization, and our sales never went anywhere.

The people who could afford our product, like the CEOs of our target customers, didn't want our solution. They simply didn't care about improving communication and feedback from their distributed workforce, and in some cases, they downright avoided it. We had failed to thoughtfully pick a buyer with purchase authority and develop a solution based on their problems.

So how do you find good buyers? Here is a quick review of some common departments at businesses. I have broken the list down between departments that generally have budgets and authority to buy things and those that do not.

Departments with significant budget and priority:

- **CEO (and board members):** If your solution solves a major problem for the CEO, it is very likely that the company will buy your product immediately. The CEO can cut all lines, eliminate all processes, and almost immediately execute anything to solve their problems. If you can understand the problems of the CEO, then you can build solutions relevant to your customer's business. The CEO, though, can also be hard to reach, so we want to engage other buyers too.
- **Marketing:** This department generally has the most money to buy things with lots of flexibility. Their job is to drive sales, which is usually the top priority for most companies.
- **Sales:** This department has money but mainly to spend on salaries for salespeople. Nevertheless, they are willing to experiment with any tool that can drive more sales faster. Given the compensation framework for most sales teams, whereby their pay and job are tied to the dollars they sell, they are motivated to move fast.

- **Product, engineering/technology, design:** It depends on the business vertical, but most businesses understand that investment in their product will lead to growth, though it may be more challenging to get the budget for products than sales or marketing.

Departments with less budget (cost centers):

- **Customer support:** Most businesses spend a lot of time trying to find ways to make support as cheap as possible. If your product saves money, they may listen, but they don't generally have significant budgets to try new things.
- **Human resources:** An incredibly important department, but often underinvested and very limited budgets for most products.
- **Operations and logistics:** Very business dependent with high variance, but again businesses are usually spending time trying to figure out how to make operations cheaper, though this can open doors for new innovative products if it's a large expense.
- **Finance:** This one can go either way. Finance is creating the budgets, after all, and if they want to give themselves some money, they often can. But it's a cost center, and they are usually frugal.

Every business is different, and a department's importance and influence in company spending could vary significantly. In almost every business, though, the chief executive officer will have the ultimate prioritization and authority. As a result, when in doubt, default to understanding and solving the CEO's problems, and you will find your solutions will be relevant and prioritized.

Create a List and Schedule Meetings with Buyers

Now that you have an idea of the market you want and have identified the buyer with purchase authority, it's time to make a target customer list and set up meetings to get their feedback.

For consumer businesses, you can easily use your survey data from the prior section (such as email addresses and phone numbers) to reach out to consumers individually and talk to them. At TapCommerce, we would just send them a personal email message and offer them a gift card for a few minutes of their time. I've found most consumers are extremely willing to chat openly for a relatively small compensation, especially if you are listening to their problems in order to help them.

For B2B businesses, it can be a little more challenging to reach your buyers. Your buyers are often quite busy. They are also quite popular, as many people are trying to sell them things. You should try and reach them any way you can, and make it very clear what you want from them.

Here are a few channels you can use to engage a busy B2B buyer:

- **LinkedIn Sales Navigator:** Sign up at linkedin.com, create a list of target customers, and send messages to get their feedback.
- **Expert networks:** Use solutions such as GLG, Tegus, and Expertwired to reach qualified buyers in just a few clicks.

- **Conferences and trade shows:** Sign up for and attend conferences for your industry. Introduce yourself to attendees, listen to panels, and learn everything you can.
- **Email outreach:** You can use tools such as ZoomInfo, Seamless.AI, Lusha, and many more to find lists of companies and individual contact information.

For the actual content of the message, be clear and to the point. Explain that you are looking to build a product for people like them, and that you would love a few minutes of their time to hear their feedback.

Put yourself in their shoes. What would make them reply to you and give you a few minutes? I would try to find common ground by learning a little about them. Did you grow up in a similar area? Go to a similar school? Do they have interests in this area? It is a bit more work to do this additional research, but it will significantly lift the percentage of people who reply to your messages.

You should expect to see about 1–5 percent of people respond to your messages. So if you send 100 messages, you may only schedule one initial meeting. Work hard and send repeated messages to try and schedule at least ten meetings for your first exploration to ensure you get an accurate market depiction. Departments with less sales outreach, like HR or operations, may be easier to reach, but it varies significantly by industry.

Getting Qualitative and Quantitative Feedback from Interviews

Once you have some meetings scheduled, you can start to learn from your buyers. Before the meeting, you should prepare a list of questions you want to ask the buyer. Below is a quick sample question structure that we have used at some of my companies. Adjust it to your needs, but let me explain why we have the structure below.

We start by confirming basics about what the person does, confirm they match with your buyer, and also build a bit of a relationship to understand them. Next, we jump into understanding their problems and those of their company. This is really the key. Based on their answers, you can then follow up with more questions to learn about the problem.

Sample Questions for Interview:

1. What is your official title and how long have you been in this role? How did you end up getting this role?
2. What are your primary responsibilities?
3. We are trying to build products to solve problems for you and people like you. What are the top three problems in your job today?
4. Can you explain more about [Insert problem #1]? Why is it a problem? What metrics are tracked that highlight this problem? What have you done to try and fix it? [Ask follow-up questions as relevant.]
5. On a scale from 1 to 10, how big of a problem is [Insert problem #1] today? (1 = a minor problem, 10 = an extremely important problem)
6. Why do you feel that way?
7. Can you explain more about [Insert problem #2]? Why is it a problem? What metrics are tracked that highlight this problem? What have you done to try and fix it? [Ask follow-up questions as relevant.]

8. On a scale from 1 to 10, how big of a problem is [Insert problem #2] today? (1 = a minor problem, 10 = an extremely important problem)
9. Why do you feel that way?
10. Can you explain more about [Insert problem #3]? Why is it a problem? What metrics are tracked that highlight this problem? What have you done to try and fix it? [Ask follow-up questions as relevant.]
11. On a scale from 1 to 10, how big of a problem is [Insert problem #3] today? (1 = a minor problem, 10 = an extremely important problem)
12. Why do you feel that way?
13. What are the top three problems for your business/place of work today? [This will be less relevant for a CEO who will have the same problems, but interesting for mid-level buyers.]
14. Why do you feel that way?
15. Can you explain more about [Insert big company problem #1, 2, 3]? Why is it a problem? What metrics does the company track to measure this problem? What has your company done to try and fix it?
16. Is there anything you would like to emphasize or anything you think we missed?
17. If you were starting a company in this industry today, what would it do?
18. Any other questions or feedback?
19. Would you be open to a follow-up conversation? What is the best way to reach you?

Before you jump straight into the interview with these questions, here are a few tactics I've found to get the most out of each interview. When a buyer responds, their first answer is often very surface level. When doing interviews, give the buyer a ton of room to talk. Ask your question, then simply don't speak for as long as possible. Let the buyer finish their thought, then wait even longer for them to come up with additional ideas and thoughts. Resist the temptation to respond, and just let them talk more until more than ten seconds of silence has passed and it's unbelievably awkward. The best information often comes at the end of the answer.

Don't bias the buyer by pushing your solution. This happens all the time and can destroy the process with false positives. It is tempting to jump straight into solutions, because you are getting excited and you really want feedback, but please do not mention anything about your solution until you have really dug in on their problems. I've done a lot of these conversations, and the minute your solution comes up, it can be a lot harder to keep a non-biased conversation going. The buyer will feel compelled to validate your solution in order to be polite.

When I was selling a mobile application tool at TapCommerce, I made the mistake of mentioning mobile apps early on when talking to some buyers. All future answers from the buyer swerved back to mobile apps. As a result, we thought that mobile apps were a really important problem for all of these buyers, but in reality they were not a top priority. The buyer was just trying to be polite and engage me in conversation that they thought was most relevant. If you can't contain your excitement to discuss your solution ideas, wait until the end of the conversation, but we will get into testing solutions in depth in the next chapter.

Finally, in addition to a written record of the conversation, I strongly advise you to record your interviews, though you should pay attention to local legalities on the consent required to record a phone call. At Attentive, we use a solution called Gong for these recordings, but you can also just use Zoom's standard recording system. Listen to the recording after you complete it, or at least read the transcript that is automatically generated by Zoom and other solutions. You can also use solutions like OpenAI to generate quick summaries for your reference to review later.

Interpreting Survey Scores

In the sample questions provided above, we offer a combination of both quantitative and qualitative responses. When trying to find a buyer problem, I want to find a problem that is extremely important to the buyer, commonly referred to as a "burning problem," which the buyer will act on urgently.

Here is a rough idea of how I think about problem scoring:

- 0–7: not a problem
- 7–8: neutral
- 8–9: a strong problem
- 9–10: a burning problem

Put another way, if the average respondent score is below an 8, you should be concerned that this problem is not a really big issue for your buyer.

Create and Refine a Problem Definition Document (PDD)

Using the information gathered through online surveys, buyer interviews, and general online research, we can create a problem definition document (PDD), which will define the buyer problems in our target market.

Below is a blank PDD template, and then a filled-out version for Attentive. The PDD is a living and breathing document. As you learn more information from your buyers, and as the market changes, you can update the PDD to reflect your best view of the current problems. By defining and refining your buyer problems in detail, it will make it a lot easier to come up with potential solutions. The answers in italics are a guide on how to fill out the answers in the template.

PDD SAMPLE TEMPLATE

Industry Name: *The name of your target industry*
Market size: *How big is your market and is it growing?*
Buyer Name(s): *Role(s) of your target buyers*

Problem #1:
Definition: *Define the problem in a few sentences.*
Metrics: *List all of the metrics related to this problem and how they are judged.*
Solutions: *List out anything the buyers have tried to solve this problem, and explain why it hasn't solved the problem today.*
Buyer(s) authority: What authority does the buyer have?
Rating: *1–10 Rating for Problem*
Problem #X . . . *Repeat for as many problems as you identify.*

PDD FOR ATTENTIVE

Industry Name: *eCommerce/Retail*
Market size: *450 Billion growing to 1.7 Trillion over next 10 years*
Buyer Name(s): *CEO, VP eCommerce, CMO, VP Marketing*

Problem #1:
Definition: *I am struggling to reach my customers and potential customers, and as a result, my revenue is not growing as fast as I want.*
Metrics showcasing problem:

- *Revenue: the revenue driven from my communication channels is not growing over time. Email marketing performance is declining.*
- *Open rate: the percentage of people that are opening my emails is going down over time.*
- *Click-through rate: the percentage of people that are clicking/engaging with my marketing communications is going down over time.*

Solutions:

- *Tried to make a mobile app, but downloads were expensive and people don't use the mobile app.*
- *Tried to run affiliate advertising, but quality was a problem, with lots of fake traffic.*
- *Tried to use Facebook Messenger, but couldn't get people to sign up.*

Buyer(s) authority: *Buyer has complete authority to spend money on solutions.*
Rating: 9.5/*10*
Problem #X . . . *Repeat for as many problems as you identify.*

Make Sure You Like the Problem

While this process may seem a bit slow, it will also teach you a ton about getting into your industry before you have committed. My mom is a pediatrician and went to medical school in Philadelphia. On the first day of school, they brought all of the students into the lab and told everyone to pair up. Everyone was then tasked with drawing a sample of blood from their partner. As I write these sentences, I get a little squeamish, and so did many of the people in class that day. As a result, a number of students dropped out of medical school in the first week of classes. While this saved those students from years of study, I'm sure they wished they had experienced this type of technical experience before taking years of undergraduate premed courses. By taking the time to talk to people in the industry and run the PDD process, you can get a better feel for your interest in the problem area and whether you want to put years or even decades of your life into solving it.

CHAPTER 2

Testing Solutions

You have identified a massive market that you are ready to work in for many years. You have spoken to dozens, if not hundreds, of potential customers, and you have created a problem definition document (PDD).You have identified a real, burning customer problem. You probably have started to have ideas to solve the problem and you think you are ready to start building solutions.

This chapter, though, is dedicated to rapidly testing solutions *without* building your product. We will run through the reasons why building a product at this stage can be dangerous. Then, we will review other ways to test your solution to see if they work. If you find a solution that truly works, then, and only then, can you jump into building your solution in the next chapter.

Principles of Testing Solutions

1. **Don't just build:** Resist the urge to make a solution without testing the concept first.
2. **Create a solution specification document (SSD):** Write a detailed overview of the solution you want to build.

3. **Turn your SSD into a pitch:** Create slides to talk to buyers about your solution.
4. **Be careful to get quality feedback:** Most buyers will not provide candid and helpful information unless you can provide an open space to listen.
5. **Get buyer feedback on your solution:** Use this template to collect objective data.
6. **Do not invest in a product until you have verified buyers:** Force yourself to presell the product and create a list of demand before you build.

Don't Just Build

Building a product too early can be very dangerous. Once you have built something, it is a lot harder to throw it away. If the thing you built doesn't solve the buyer problem, then you can find yourself as a solution in search of a problem. This is the most common problem I've seen, and I've experienced it firsthand many times in my career.

When I was a few years out of school, I was living in New York, and I loved sorbet. I was on a quest to find the best sorbet in town, but there was no definitive list to find it. As a result, my cofounder and I decided to make a website dedicated to making it easy to search restaurant menus, which we called Hungry4. We walked all around town and collected hundreds of menus. We typed the menus into an online database, spent a while making it searchable, and designed a complicated interface to search the menus. After months of work, we started showing it to people. Our consumer didn't really understand the search by menu. Instead, they wanted a map of restaurants, and the ability to easily order food online. We had devoted so much time to our angle that we didn't listen and just kept refining our product. After a few months, our energy ran out, and we set it aside.

If instead we had interviewed buyers more about our solution, we would have found out they weren't interested. Furthermore, we would have heard what they did want—food delivered fast from a wide variety of restaurants throughout the world. If we had listened earlier on, then we could have helped build unicorn businesses like DoorDash, Postmates, or Uber Eats.

Resist the impulse to just build. Make it a rule that actually making the product is the last step, and you want to do everything else you can before making the product. Everything else is a lot easier to do and much easier to throw away if it isn't working.

Create a Solution Specification Document (SSD)

A solution specification document (SSD) is the blueprint for developing and testing your product idea. You will use your SSD to help create more documents to explain your idea to buyers and get their feedback. Based on their feedback, you can refine the document until it becomes something you are ready to build.

If you have completed your problem definition document (PDD) in the last chapter, then creating your solution specification document (SSD) will be easy. It is a continuation of the PDD. After restating your core buyer problems, you will define your solution in detail and make additional documents to communicate that solution to buyers.

Below, I have reproduced our sample PDD for Attentive from the prior chapter, then I've added a new section to make the SSD. Below this sample, I have also included a template to create your own PDD/SSD.

PDD + SSD FOR ATTENTIVE

Industry Name: *eCommerce/Retail*
Market size: *450 billion growing to 1.7 trillion over next ten years*
Buyer Name(s): *CEO, VP eCommerce, CMO, VP Marketing*

Problem #1:
Definition: *I am struggling to reach my customers and potential customers, and as a result, my revenue is not growing as fast as I want.*
Metrics showcasing problem:

- *Revenue: the revenue driven from my communication channels is not growing over time. Email marketing performance is declining.*
- *Open rate: the percentage of people that are opening my emails is going down over time.*
- *Click-through rate: the percentage of people that are clicking/engaging with my marketing communications is going down over time.*

Solutions:

- *Tried to make a mobile app, but downloads were expensive, and people don't use it*

- *Tried to run affiliate advertising, but quality was a problem*
- *Tried to use Facebook Messenger, but couldn't get people to sign up*

Buyer(s) authority: *Buyer has complete authority to spend money on solutions*
Rating: 9.5/*10*

Solution:

Description: Create a new way to help ecommerce and retail businesses to reach their customers and drive more revenue using text messaging (SMS).
Metrics of Success:

- *Sign-up rate: Measure the percentage of consumers that sign up to get text messages.*
- *Open rate: Measure the percentage of SMS text messages that a consumer reads.*
- *Click-through rate: Measure the percentage of SMS text message links that a consumer clicks.*
- *Revenue: Measure the amount of revenue driven by SMS messages.*

Minimum Product Requirements to test the metrics (each requirement matches a metric):

- *System to get consumers to sign up for text messages, which measures the rate of consumers that sign up based on the number of consumers given the opportunity to sign up*
- *System for sending a text message to the list of active subscribers, with the ability to measure the open rate, click-through rate, and revenue driven from a message*

Potential Challenges

- *Businesses do not currently have SMS marketing programs. Are they willing to try them?*
- *Consumers do not typically sign up for SMS marketing programs. Are they willing to sign up? Can we get a lot of them to sign up?*

PDD SAMPLE TEMPLATE

Industry Name: *The name of your target industry*
Market size: *How big is your market and is it growing?*
Buyer Name(s): *Role(s) of your target buyers*

Problem #1:

Definition: *Define the problem in a few sentences.*
Metrics: *List all of the metrics related to this problem and how they are judged.*
Solutions: *List out anything the buyers have tried to solve this problem, and explain why it hasn't solved the problem today.*
Buyer(s) authority: *What authority does the buyer have?*
Rating: *1–10 Rating for Problem*

Solution:

Description: *State in one sentence how your solution will solve the buyer problem. Be careful to use terms the buyer will understand.*
Metrics of Success:

- Metric #1: *Explain the metric you want to impact based on the metric in the problem above.*
- Metric #2: *Explain for an additional metric.*

Minimum Product Requirements to Test Metrics:

- *List the product elements you will need to build to test your metrics of success.*
- *As a rule of thumb, each line item should match each metric you want to measure. Any line item that doesn't measure to a metric should be closely scrutinized.*

Potential Challenges

- *List each challenge you foresee occurring with your product.*
- *You will add to this list as you pitch customers for feedback and hear their concerns.*

Turn Your SSD into a Pitch

Using your initial PDD and SSD, you can now create a short presentation to pitch your product to potential buyers. For B2C businesses (like a new type of soda), you can directly pitch consumers. For B2B (like a new business software), you can pitch the business decision-makers.

I have found success breaking the pitch down into the basic components represented in your PDD/SSD:

- Overview—what the company does
- Problem/trends—the core buyer problem(s)
- Solution/product—what your product does
- Getting started—next steps to try your product, and an opportunity for feedback

Below is an early Attentive pitch, along with a script for presenting it and an explanation of each slide. It's usually easier to get feedback if you keep the pitch relatively short (fewer than twenty slides) with minimal text. While your pitch will change over time, we have used this core structure for the entire life of Attentive, all the way to over 8,000 customers and hundreds of millions in revenue. I hope it helps give you some ideas for your own deck.

Cover Slide:

Script:

Thanks again for your time. At Attentive, we are building a new way to reach your customers and drive tons of incremental sales with text messaging.

Explanation:

This was our initial cover slide. Optimally, this cover slide says what your company does and how it will solve the buyer's problem. At the time we went to market, SMS (text messaging) was seen as very uncool, so we are angling toward a reinvention angle, and we probably overdid it. This slide failed to include the buyer's problem. If I did it again, I would say,

"Drive more revenue with a new, universal marketing channel"

"Mobile messaging built for huge ROI"

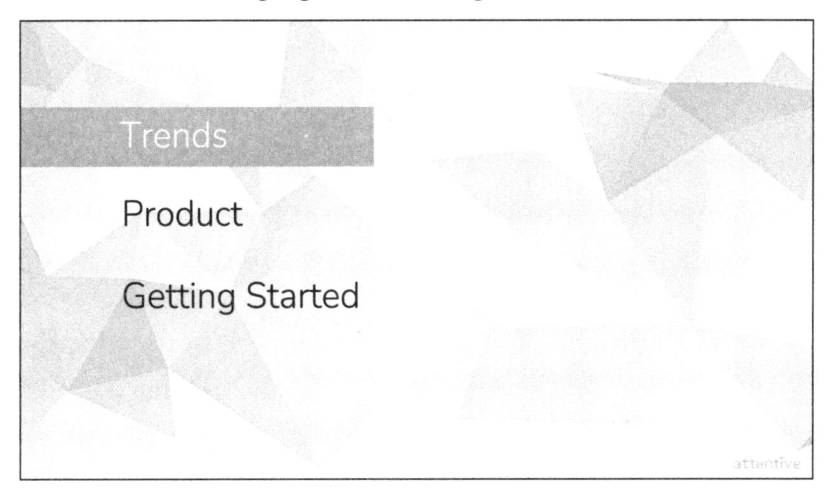

Script:

Today, I'm going to take you through a very brief presentation.

- *First—we will go through the TRENDS that are driving the growth of messaging marketing;*
- *Second—we will dig into how our product is capitalizing on those trends;*
- *Third—we will show you how easy it is to try out our solution;*
- *Sound good? Great, let's get started.*

Explanation:

This slide is optional, but I personally always like to have an agenda to let the buyer know where we will go in the meeting. I've found this keeps them engaged and feeling in control.

In this agenda, a few notes on the section names:

- Trends: This is our problem section. I call it "trends," because it focuses on the analytical aspects of our problem's metrics, and it also helps strike a more neutral to positive tone, rather than "problems," which starts the presentation in a negative manner.
- Product: This is our solution section. Calling it "product" just helps it appear a bit less forced and salesy, whereas "solution" is a bit forceful and abrasive in my opinion.
- Get started: What does the buyer need to try out your product or service? By ending with "getting started," we can let them know your expectations, and see if they are willing to do it.

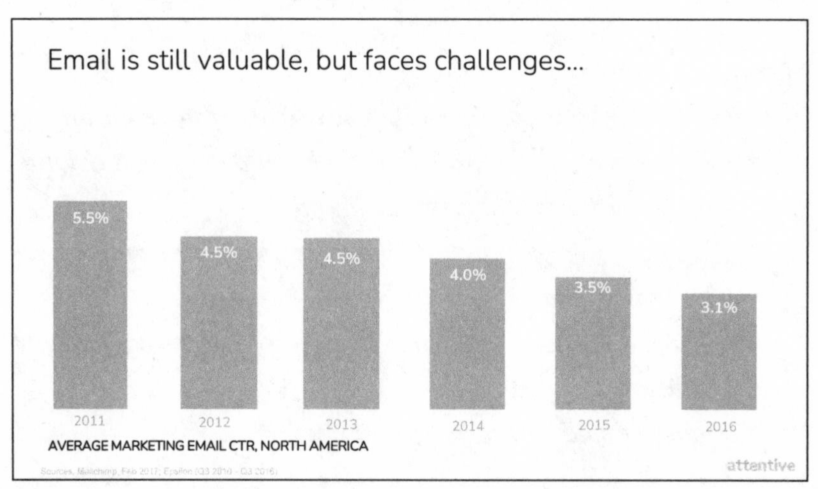

Script:

It is really hard to be a CMO or CEO at an ecommerce business. Your top way of communicating and reaching your customers, email, is down by almost half in the last six years. When you see a chart like this, you have a good idea where it will be in a few years, even further down. Marketers need to find a new way to reach their customers.

Explanation:
Earlier in the PDD, we defined the core problem as, "*I am struggling to reach my customers and potential customers, and as a result, my revenue is not growing as fast as I want. Revenue: the revenue driven from my communication channels is not growing over time. Email marketing performance is declining. Open rate: the percentage of people that are opening my emails is going down over time. Click-through rate: the percentage of people that are clicking/engaging with my marketing communications is going down over time.*"

In this slide, we are taking this problem, translating it into a chart of data, and telling the story to the buyer with the data. It is a good sign if you see a lot of agreement and head nodding during the problem section of the slide. This slide has worked very well for us, and some version of it has been updated and used for most of our history.

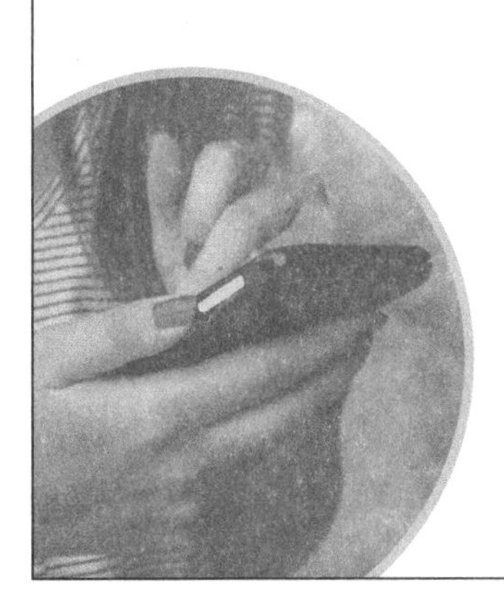

Solution Bridge Slide:

Script:

SMS Mobile messaging is an incredible channel that is extremely underutilized by companies today. Think about it. . . . You open almost every message you get, and you click on a ton of the links you are sent. This is 10X better than the performance you are seeing from email.

Explanation:

I like to include a transition slide between the problem and the solution. This slide bridges the two areas with a data point that leans in the direction of our solution without directly saying the solution itself.

Solution Slide:

Script:

Attentive gives you everything you need to build your mobile messaging channel and send messages that drive lots of incremental revenue. With Attentive, you can sign consumers up using our two-tap sign-up, customize the messages they want, send messages to your subscribers, and measure your program to improve performance.

Explanation:
This is the most important slide or set of slides in the deck. Through your prior research, you feel pretty good about your customer problem, but you don't know if your solution solves that problem. The purpose of this deck is to get feedback from the customer on your solution. In this example, we had one initial slide, but we eventually broke this out into four more slides that explain in detail each of these product features. You need to get feedback on each feature to understand what is essential and what can be cut from your initial product. This is the area of the deck that will adapt the most over time.

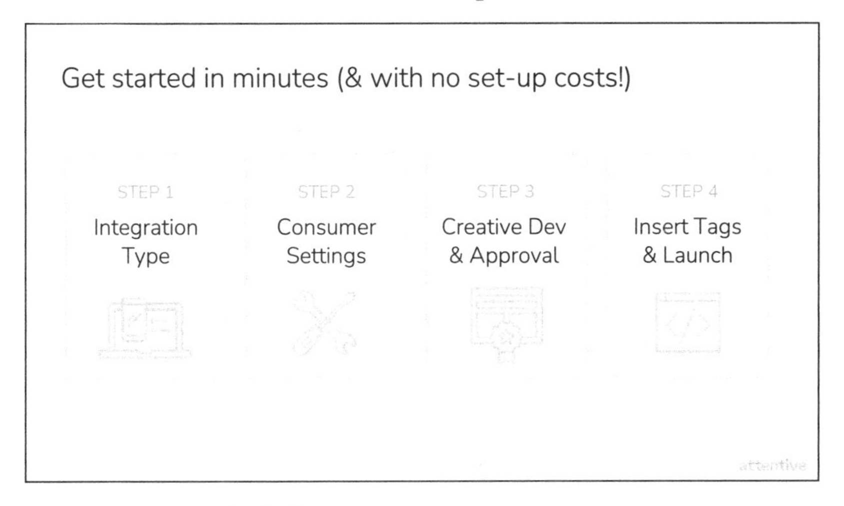

Getting Started Slide:
Script:
Getting started with Attentive is easy. All you need to do is integrate Attentive on your mobile website by adding our JavaScript tag, approve our sign-up units, and you are ready to launch.

Explanation:
Clearly lay out what you need the buyer to do in order to try out your product. This will help you to prioritize the products you build, and also to understand any major blocking items to getting your minimum viable product off the ground.

Now you have everything you need to make your own solution pitch deck. You can use this deck to see if buyers want to try your solution. You should also be developing a waiting list of customers that have verbally agreed to try your product, which we will cover later in this chapter.

Be Careful to Get Quality Feedback

Before you start pitching, it's important to understand something about people. Very few people will give you critical feedback. People are inherently nonconfrontational, polite, and absorbed in their own world. If you pitch someone your business idea, they are very likely to give you encouraging remarks, regardless of their true opinion. In most cases, people won't completely understand or care about your business. In some cases, they may even outright lie to avoid confrontation.

You need to learn how to gather the grains of truth from each person you pitch. Even better, you must uncover the very few people that are willing to give candid, intelligent, and overtly critical feedback. That feedback is the most valuable thing your business can find.

Step back for a minute and imagine the experience of the buyer. You are asked by the founder of a company, who may be a friend of yours, to hear the pitch for their business. The founder excitedly tells you about their company. It is really hard and risky to give negative advice. The founder may get angry and take actions that potentially adversely hurt the buyer. On the other hand, giving positive feedback is really easy. The founder will be very appreciative of your time, and likely look to help you in the future.

I've given thousands of business pitches, and I struggle to think of an instance in which I was given direct negative feedback without considerable prying. The next section will teach you how to get that critical feedback by conducting an open conversation and asking specific questions to truly measure interest.

How to Get Buyer Feedback on Your Solution

You have put in a lot of work, and you are really excited to start building your solution, so you really hope customers love your solution. You need to avoid your confirmation bias. Confirmation bias, as defined by Nickerson, is "the tendency to interpret new evidence as confirmation of one's existing beliefs or theories."[3] Keep your excitement, but be skeptical that your solution will actually work. Create a system to get credible feedback on your solution.

In order to get objective feedback, consider using the template below to score your solution. This is done in a similar style to our questions about the buyer problem, so you should be comfortable with this flow.

---

3 Nickerson, Raymond S. 1998. "Confirmation Bias: A Ubiquitous Phenomenon in Many Guises." *Review of General Psychology* 2 (2): 175–220. pages.ucsd.edu/~mckenzie/nickersonConfirmationBias.pdf.

Post-Pitch Verbal Survey

1. How much is X problem an issue in your work/life? (Rate 1–10)
   Rating: 1: It is not an issue at all; 10: It's a very important problem.
2. Why do you feel that way?
   Open-form answer
3. How interested would you be in X solution for this problem (break out solutions if more than one)?
   Rating: 1: Not at all; 10: Very interested
4. Why do you feel that way?
   Open-form answer
5. What do you like the most about this solution?
   Open-form answer
6. What do you wish was different about this solution?
   Open-form answer
7. What other things have you tried to solve this problem?
   Open-form answer; can make list once you get a lot of replies
8. How would you rate your satisfaction with (insert alternate competitor solution)?
   Rating: 1: Not at all satisfied; 10: Very satisfied
9. Why do you feel that way?
   Open-form answer

Earlier in this section, I provided some guidance on how to interpret the ratings to your buyer's problem. Similar to analyzing the problem, I would apply the following table to the average scores you receive for the solution:

- 0–7: does not solve the problem

- 7–8: might solve the problem
- 8–9: most likely solves the problem
- 9–10: definitely solves the problem

So if you are getting an average score below a 6, you should be very concerned that the solution you developed is unlikely to be adopted by the buyer. On the other hand, if you find a score approaching 10, you can get pretty excited, because your buyers may immediately buy your product.

Do Not Invest in a Product Until You Have Verified Buyers

With one of my earliest businesses, we thought people wanted a tool to build a mobile application for their online store. We had a few engineers, so we just started building. Over the course of a few months, we built all the components that a mobile app needed to be successful. At the same time, I started selling the product to potential customers. Our engineering team had a full product built and ready to go, but we couldn't convince a single business to use it, even when we were giving it away for free. We ended up having to throw away all of the code, and we lost one of our nine startup lives. Some of our investors stopped asking about our business, and one of them stopped showing up to board meetings.

Resist the urge to build a product before you have committed buyers. I have personally made this mistake many times, and I've seen many entrepreneurs make it. It's a terrible experience to spend a lot of time and money to build something, release it to the world, and find out that no one wants it. Your team will become demotivated, and struggle to move on. Make sure you have committed buyers before you build.

CHAPTER 3

Building Your Solution

You have already done all of your homework to maximize the success rate of your product. You defined your core problem, and tested solutions by talking to dozens if not hundreds of buyers. You have a list of initial committed customers, and it's time to build your first product.

This chapter will focus on how to build your first product as fast as possible. We will look for ways to massively cut from your original product spec and build the absolute minimum initial product to launch. After launch, we want you to live and breathe with your customers to closely understand what they love about your product, and what they wish was different. We will also encourage you to hold off for as long as possible on "going social" with your product launch, retaining the most optionality on pivoting based on the feedback you receive.

Principles of Building Your Solution

1. **Cut 50 percent of your minimum viable product (MVP):** Decide what you want to build for your initial product, then cut the features and product in half so you can test and learn faster.

2. **How to launch your product off the ground:** Create a snowball from one customer to hundreds.
3. **Executives should do customer support:** Your cofounders need to be embedded with customers at every stage in the business to understand what's working.
4. **Don't go social:** Hold back the temptation to tell the world about your new venture. The benefits are often short term, and the negatives can ruin your business.

Cut 50 Percent of Your Minimum Viable Product (MVP)

In the prior chapter, you created a solution specification document (SSD). After many customer conversations, you have refined that document into something you are now ready to build into a real product. Building a product can be very expensive. For your initial product, reduce your specification to the minimum viable product (MVP) that you can build, and then cut an additional 50 percent of the features to further simplify it. Only build the features that will test whether your product can achieve the metrics (as defined in your SSD) to solve your buyer's problem. While many items may seem essential, if you force yourself to the absolute smallest product, you will find that some features are completely unnecessary, and you've saved a lot of time and money not building them all. If many customers start screaming for the feature, then you can build it.

In 2017, I completed dozens of customer pitches for Attentive, our text message marketing business. After many customer conversations, we made an initial list of the capabilities of the minimum viable product in order to take the product to market.

Initial Minimum Viable Product

1. **Get consumer SMS sign-ups:** SMS consumer sign-up unit for mobile websites (test sign-up rate)
2. **Measure sign-up performance:** Analytics for consumer sign-up unit (test sign-up rate)
3. **Send SMS messages:** Web application for creating and sending SMS messages
4. **Track message performance:** Web link creation system for creating and measuring message performance (test click-through rate, and revenue driven)
5. **Display message performance:** Web application for viewing message performance

This initial MVP could have taken more than 120 days to complete. We had customers who wanted to launch immediately, and we also wanted to learn from customers before building anything that they may not like or use. We needed to remove features.

This removal process will likely be very painful if you have multiple cofounders and closely involved team members. As you define your product, different team members will be emotionally excited and connected to specific features. Removing those features will be like removing their contribution. This emotion is to be expected, and frankly, if you don't have this type of heated discussion, you probably aren't cutting enough.

Two suggestions to make the process smoother: First, remind people that anything cut can simply be added in the weeks or months after launch, a very small amount of time in the grand scheme of things; second, consider having one person who has complete authority for making the product spec list and who is also responsible for hitting your goals on launching your product.

At Attentive, we ultimately had one person who made the final decision on what was included or not, and that was my cofounder, Andrew, who ran our product development. Andrew understood the goal was to get a product out the door as fast as possible, and he was responsible for hitting that time line. He evaluated each item in our list and focused on cutting things that were nonessential, especially anything that would take longer to build. After a day or two of debates, we were able to cut a tremendous amount of features with a revised MVP.

Revised 50 percent + Cut

1. **Get consumer SMS sign-ups:** SMS consumer sign-up unit for mobile websites.
2. **Measure sign-up performance:** Analytics for consumer sign-up unit—Replaced with manual Excel sheet of data emailed to customer.
3. **Send SMS messages:** Web application for creating and sending SMS messages—Replaced with manual email between our engineers and the customer.
4. **Track message performance:** Web link creation system for creating and measuring message performance—Replaced with Google Analytics tracking link, removing the need for the creation of our own measurement links.

5. **Display message performance:** Web application for viewing message performance—Replaced with manual Excel sheet of data emailed to customer.

After these changes and removals, we were able to make an initial product in a matter of weeks. Customers were able to go live with our product and give us invaluable feedback that helped us build the right products as our business progressed.

To maximize the effectiveness of your initial product time line, point the entire company at getting the initial test live. During this stage it's important that your team is comfortable working as generalists doing whatever it takes to get the MVP live as soon as possible. The product manager (who is likely a cofounder) should own defining the scope and requirements of the MVP and liaising with early test customers to keep them informed of progress and to ensure that customers are lined up ready to test once the MVP is ready.

How to Launch Your Product Off the Ground

While consumer-based businesses may find it easy to get customers to try a product, B2B businesses can be very hard to launch. On many occasions, I have seen customers drop out at the last minute, and all of a sudden you don't have anyone to try your product.

With Attentive, we took a few steps that were successful in getting off the ground. First, we recruited several customers to our first batch to try our product. Through the launch process, we lost a customer or two, but we were still able to successfully launch with the remaining businesses. Don't overexpose your business to one pilot customer, but instead spread out the risk to ensure you get off the ground.

Second, during the initial launch months of the business, we held a daily stand-up across our entire company. In the stand-up meeting, everyone actually stood up at their desk and provided a quick update on what they did that day and what they planned to do the next day. This helped to ensure alignment across the entire company working together toward our goal of the product launch.

Third, we also brought our customers into our product development process. We set up a weekly check-in call. In the call, we would walk through the results for the prior week, new product elements we had changed or added, and what we planned to build in the next week. We asked customers for feedback on features, even if for a few minutes to give feedback on a design. This type of engagement helped us to make better products, but it also helped our customers to feel committed to our work together. Making them part of the process also made them part of the team and tied them to our ultimate success.

Executives Should Do Customer Support

Your partnership and relationship with the buyer should not end when your product goes live. Instead, the founding team should be doing customer support when you are getting off the ground, and stay close to support until the company is at massive scale. Even then, it should never stop, as buyer problems and needs will change over time.

With Attentive, our head of product worked with our head of customer success to manage all of our first fifty customers directly. This included every step of the customer life cycle, and all the steps the customers took to use our products. We had weekly meetings, ongoing lunches and dinners, and seasonal events. At all of these activities, we worked to build trust and truly understand what they were feeling. These meetings were often more productive in person, especially in a non-work setting, as your best information may come at dessert, or at the bar around the corner at night, when truth flows more freely.

We made one of the most important decisions in the company history through one of these conversations. I was at the office of one of our early customers. We had just run through some performance data late on a Thursday afternoon. We had also brought along a bottle of rosé wine to congratulate them, and we all decided to have a drink and hang out a bit. During that hangout, the customer asked me how fast the business was growing. I explained that the product worked really well, but that customers often didn't have the budget flexibility to try out our solution. We had experimented with a brief free trial, but sometimes this didn't last long enough to show success. The customer simply suggested, "Why would you not give the product out for free for everyone to try until they see success? It almost always works, right?" It sounds like a simple idea, but at the time companies in our space did not offer long free trials. We adopted a lengthy free trial strategy the next day, and sales quickly skyrocketed.

Don't "Go Social"

You are excited about your new business, and you want to tell the world. You consider updating your LinkedIn with your new company, posting about it on social networks, and telling all your family and friends what you are doing. I *strongly recommend* keeping quiet for as long as possible. The negatives of publishing your work will likely outweigh the positives. Here are a few things I have experienced.

First, by telling your network of friends and colleagues, you will lose flexibility to pivot and change your business. For the first few times I started a company, I would tell my family, friends, and close work colleagues. It was fun to talk about when starting, but painful to explain when it failed or pivoted to something else. I found myself constantly updating and explaining to skeptical bystanders.

Second, by publishing anything you tell the world about your idea. Each business I have founded has been inundated with copycats shortly after we announced our first fundraising. New businesses have gotten much easier to create. You can build products fast with less money by using smart tools and sales-first processes. That's what this book is all about, after all. When you are early on, your competitive advantage is significantly less than it will be in six months or twelve months later. Consider it your head start in the race. Why give up advantage for the work you have done to find the problem and design the solution? I like to keep quiet for as long as humanly possible.

CHAPTER 4

Recognizing Product Market Fit

Congratulations! You have reached an incredible achievement and built the early stages of a working business. You recognized a real customer problem, built a great initial product, and have a steady stream of customer growth. Is your business ready to grow a lot faster? Have you found the big business of your dreams?

The life of a startup company can be divided into two stages: before product market fit, and after product market fit. Before product market fit, entrepreneurs will carefully conserve capital, limit any long-term commitments, and quickly change their products and positioning to find a winner. After product market fit, the growth-minded entrepreneur will scale as fast as possible to grab share as fast as possible. They want to become the market leader.

In this chapter, we will review some helpful tests to determine if your business has achieved product market fit. We will also provide tools to verify that your core unit economics will work, and finish with a few stumbling blocks to keep an eye on. If you pass the tests, you are ready to scale!

Principles of Recognizing Product Market Fit

1. **Tests for product market fit:** Consider these qualifications before you vastly grow your operations.
2. **Verify unit economics before you scale:** Make sure your business makes money before you scale.
3. **Common stumbling blocks to scaling:** Know the issues that can pop up when you try to expand your footprint.

Tests for Product Market Fit

Achieving product market fit is a huge milestone to significant business expansion. This usually comes with large investments in new employees, production, and marketing. It can be very dangerous to make these investments too early and find you aren't yet hitting product market fit. You will end up needing to fire employees, waste resources, and potentially doom your business.

So what do we look for to see if a business has product market fit? Here are some indicators to keep in mind:

Testing the Metrics from Your SDD

Earlier in this section, you wrote out a solution definition document, in which you defined the metrics that impact your problem. You now have built a minimum product to try and move those metrics. Is your solution succeeding?

With Attentive, we wanted to improve four core metrics. Our principal bar was to outperform the performance of email marketing as the closest replacement for our channel.

Below is a summary of each and the results we saw in order to feel like we were solving the customer problem:

- *Sign-up rate: Measure the percentage of consumers that sign up to get text messages. In email marketing, about 3 percent of customers signed up for an email. For SMS, our goal was to see over 1 percent of customers sign up. We didn't think consumers would be as willing, but SMS would make more money per subscriber to make up the difference. In testing, we saw over 5 percent of consumers sign up. SUCCESS.*
- *Open rate: Measure the percentage of SMS text messages that a consumer reads. Email was around 10 percent. For SMS, we were not able to measure open rate, but when we surveyed consumers we found most people opened all their SMS. SUCCESS.*
- *Click-through rate: Measure the percentage of SMS text message links that a consumer clicks. At the time we went to market, about 3 percent of consumers clicked on the email marketing messages they received. Our goal was to exceed 10 percent to significantly outperform email. Our results showed over 10 percent performance. SUCCESS.*
- *Revenue: Measure the amount of revenue driven from SMS messages. We wanted to be able to drive more revenue per subscriber than email. With our messages, we saw over 10X more revenue per subscriber. SUCCESS.*

With these results, we felt great about the ability for our product to solve the customer problem, even though many customers were still skeptical of the new channel of SMS. As a result, we made significant investments to scale our business, and over the next several years we grew into defining the market category.

Net Promoter Score (NPS)

Does your solution solve the customer problem? If it solves the customer problem, then you should have extremely happy customers who decide to continue using your product and recommend it to others.

To track this metric, consider running surveys on your current customers to find your net promoter score (NPS). The net promoter score is a single question: "How likely is it that you would recommend this company to a friend or colleague? (0–10)" Responses from 0 to 6 are considered detractors, 7 and 8 are passive, and 9 and 10 are promoters. To calculate your score, subtract the percentage from detractors from the percentage of promoters. For instance, if you have 70 percent promoters and 10 percent detractors, then your NPS would be a 60, which is excellent. NPS scores vary by industry, falling somewhere between 20 and 70. If your score is below your industry average, then you have more work to do before your solution is solving the customer problem.

For TapCommerce, we sent an automated email NPS survey to customers after thirty days of using the product. Our NPS was over 60, meaning that we had a tremendous amount of promoters and very few detractors. The average software NPS is typically around a 40, so over 50 was best in class.

Churn Rate

Another way to measure your ability to solve a customer problem is measuring the churn rate for your business. The churn rate measures the number of customers who stop using your product. For instance, if you sell a software solution, it's the number of customers that cancel their software subscription. If you sell clothing, it's the number of customers who decide not to make additional purchases from you. Churn can be a harder metric to use because it takes more time to measure, but it's also an absolute measure of success, whereas a survey result, like NPS, can be misleading if the respondents change their opinion over time.

Back in the early part of my startup career, I worked at a startup that sold lead generation. We signed up about $100K in new customer revenue each month, but we also lost about 5–10 percent in revenue each month. Customers saw diminishing returns from using our product over time, and most customers eventually stopped using it. A high churn rate is like trying to fill a bucket with holes in it. The bucket is constantly leaking and you are always fighting yourself to scale your business. It's frustrating for everyone at the company to watch as you lose each customer you fought hard to get.

Investors pay very close attention to churn rates because if a business can't fix their churn, they will stop growing and ultimately fail to scale. Additionally, since every market is finite to some degree, if you have a high churn rate, you will eventually churn your entire market and run out of room for new customers. This is what happened to that lead generation startup; we eventually ran out of the low-hanging fruit (easy accounts to buy our product), and sales became harder and harder. Our churn rate surpassed our new revenue rate, and eventually our revenue went to zero.

Inability to Keep Up with Demand

Another way to look for product market fit is to check for the ratio between the demand for your product and the supply you can provide. In an ideal situation, you should scale up your operations in order to meet a backlog of demand for your product. For example, you have a startup selling bikes. You can make five bikes per day, but you are getting orders for ten bikes per day. You need to add more resources so you can make more bikes to meet the demand otherwise you will fail to meet the needs of these customers.

In reality, for many types of business, though, you often need to scale some component of your business to test and reach additional demand. With my company Franklin, we hired a large sales and development team early on to build the product. When demand for our product failed to grow, we had a lot of overhead costs, and needed to lay off some members of our team.

When it came time to expand the business again, we first invested in non-headcount-related strategies that offered more flexible ways to manage our growth. For example, we hired consultants on monthly contracts, increased our spend on digital advertising channels, and hired full-time employees only when absolutely critical to meet our growth.

Ability to Create a Profit-Loss Forecast

The North Star of product market fit is to be able to accurately predict significant and sustained business growth over a medium to long period of time. That prediction begins with creating an operating model for your business, a profit-loss forecast.

The profit-loss is the best quick summary of your business performance over a period of time. It typically includes your overall revenue, costs to provide your service, your gross profit, operating expenses, and your overall operating profit. If any of these terms is scaring you, that's totally fine. Take a few hours to read the basics of financial accounting. The most useful class I took in business school was introduction to accounting. It should be required for all undergraduate students to encourage financial literacy.

For my first company, TapCommerce, I didn't spend a lot of time or effort creating our profit-loss forecast. My view, which was pretty popular among entrepreneurs at the time, was that financial forecasts were great for late-stage businesses, but a waste of time for early-stage businesses. As a result, we slapped together a financial forecast ahead of a fundraising event. Our model was extremely basic and wouldn't hold up to much financial scrutiny. As a result, some investors didn't take us seriously, and those who did paid a significantly cheaper price to invest. We ended up significantly overachieving the forecast, but that was largely due to the simplicity and inaccuracy of our financial model. I failed to understand that the forecasted numbers are the goals you are committing to achieving to your investors for the next year or two.

For my second business, Attentive, I had come to appreciate the importance of a thoughtful and credible financial forecast at an early stage. We spent several weeks developing a model based on our customer activity, expected sales output, retention, hiring, and many other important elements. This process helped us to pay closer attention to the levers that impacted our business performance and to change our operations. Additionally, investors respected the numbers and process we presented, and we received many investment offers at great prices.

To feel good about your future financial picture when scaling your business, you should be able to create a forecasted profit-loss over the next year or two. The assumptions should be based on real data, and should be conservative so that you feel reasonably capable in delivering the results. It's much easier to speed up your operations if you are beating goals than to slow things down.

Verify Unit Economics Before You Scale

Some of the biggest headlines around failed startups can be tracked to poor unit economics. The business achieves product market fit, grows to a large scale, but fails to make money and ultimately goes out of business. Why does this happen?

In simplest terms, a business will go bankrupt if it costs the company more money to acquire customers and provide their product than the profit they make from customers. You would think it would be pretty easy to tell if a company makes money, but in the short to medium term of a startup when you are investing a lot of capital into future revenue, it can be pretty tricky. Thankfully, we have a number of calculations you can do to find out if your business will be long-term profitable: customer acquisition cost (CAC), cost of goods sold (COGS), and customer lifetime value (LTV). These calculations are most used in software businesses, but can be applied to most business types to estimate the viability of the enterprise.

Customer Acquisition Cost (CAC)

CAC is the amount a business spends in order to acquire a new customer. For instance, if your business is selling bikes, your CAC would be all costs associated with sales and marketing of your bikes, such as: Google Ads for bike sales, salaries to your marketing team for running your Google Ads, software to run your website to process bike sales, and more. Let's say you spent $1,000 per month on all of these costs, and you sold ten bikes to ten customers, then your CAC would be $100.

A low CAC early in the life of your company is a great sign of product-market fit. It means you aren't spending a lot of money to drive each new sale, so getting more sales will likely not be very expensive. So what is a low CAC? I'd estimate it to be < 10 percent the cost of your product, but will vary based on the margin of the product you sell. Low-margin products need lower CACs to be profitable.

You should also consider breaking out your customer acquisition costs into different subgroups of your customers, called cohorts. For instance, with Attentive we divide our customers into five different customer tiers. Tier 1 customers are massive businesses that may spend seven or even eight figures with us each year. On the other hand, tier 5 businesses are very small and may not spend more than ten thousand dollars.

We use different types of marketing to reach the tier 1 "enterprise" customers than to reach the much smaller tier 5 customers. This is important because you may find your business is efficient in reaching certain cohorts and highly unprofitable in reaching others, and thus you need to adjust your operations accordingly and focus where your business is profitable.

Costs of Goods Sold (COGS)

COGS is all costs needed in order to produce your product for the customer. To continue our bike example, it would be all the costs for the raw materials to make the bikes, plus the costs associated with the labor to construct, test, and ship the bikes to the customer.

COGS can change quickly over time. In some markets, the costs can rapidly rise or fall based on market costs for raw materials or services. It's important to understand the underlying costs to create your products so you won't be surprised when the market changes.

Customer Lifetime Value (LTV)

LTV is how much total net profit a customer generates for the entire term for which they are your customer. This is an important calculation, because many businesses may not profit the first time a customer buys something from them, but they can make a lot of money from additional purchases. To calculate LTV, simply add up all of the gross sales against a customer for their entire time period as a customer, then subtract the COGS for that customer for their entire life cycle.

For example, at Attentive, our average customer will use our service for many years, producing a high lifetime value. If for some reason, though, a customer decides to stop using Attentive after only a month or two, then we would lose money by serving that customer. Our business needs to ensure we focus on customers who will work with us for long enough that they are profitable to our business.

Lifetime value can be hard to calculate, because it can take a long time to determine how much a customer is willing to spend with your business over the course of many years. You can make some initial assumptions for your business, but it's important to update them as you get more data on your customers. For instance, I may calculate that a customer will work with Attentive for an average of five years. If after seven years, though, we still have most of our customers, then I need to increase the average in our calculations.

Calculating LTV/CAC

Putting together all of these calculations, a simple way to test the strength of your business is to see how much you make per customer divided by how much it costs to acquire new customers. This is the primary measurement testing whether your business can be profitable at scale over the long term, which is what every business hopes to achieve.

A good ratio for LTV/CAC varies a lot by industry, but every industry will want to see a number that is greater than one. In many industries, the target is to see a number greater than three. The larger the number, the more your business will feel comfortable to increase your marketing spend or overall business operations while also ensuring your business is profitable.

Common Stumbling Blocks to Scaling

As your business begins to take off, there are a multitude of ways to get into trouble quickly. Here are some of the common issues I've encountered along the way after having some initial product market success:

The Buyer Total Addressable Market Is Actually Not Very Big

At TapCommerce, we were building solutions for businesses that own and operate a mobile application for an iPhone or

Android phone. This sounded like a very big market, and our initial market size estimates were huge. We estimated that we could sell our product to over 10,000+ businesses, a market exceeding $10 billion in revenue over the next decade.

After selling our product to a variety of customers, though, we realized our products were effective only for businesses with very large mobile application audiences. As a result, the number of businesses we could sell to was more like ~500 businesses globally, or roughly 5 percent of our initial target estimate. We needed to find a way to expand our product quickly to reach a larger audience, or we would run out of room for growth. This factor was one of the reasons we decided to sell the business to Twitter only two years after starting the business.

The Buyer Problem Is Temporary, and Will Go Away

The market is incredibly dynamic, and as a result some buyer problems pop up with profound strength and size, only to quickly reduce to nothing. In the first chapter on problem hunting, we showed charts that identified the CBD market as one of the fastest growing revenue industries in America in 2023. CBD is a relatively new industry that has also benefited from recently relaxed regulations, so there is a gold rush for people to build new businesses to meet demand.

In a few years, though, this market may be quickly saturated and significantly slow its growth. Furthermore, consumers may grow tired of the novelty of a new product, and sales could slump significantly. If your business is booming, continually ask yourself how your buyer's problem is changing and how that could disrupt your business.

Part 2
Culture

For most of my startup career, I thought that company cultural values were mostly bullshit. Many tech companies espouse the same values, but in practice, actually working at the company is very different. When candidates asked about culture, I often just mentioned that we worked very hard, also had a good time, and then referenced all the great perks like free lunch and crazy off-sites.

As my businesses have grown over time, though, I've come to realize how important clear cultural values can be when done right. Culture is essential toward helping any employee make small and large decisions in their workday. As you get bigger, management can't weigh in on most decisions. Culture helps your team to make their own decisions and stops behavior that could severely harm the company.

Beyond just values, culture is also the processes by which you run the business. Culture can help employees decide how to prioritize their time and how they request the time of their peers. It also sets the rules of communication across the company.

In this section, we will detail some of the steps to consider when building your company's foundational culture, including your mission and vision, and then dig into the processes you can maintain to spread and enforce that culture. We will also review ways you can see that culture in your physical work environment, benefits, and activities outside of the office.

CHAPTER 5
Creating and Reinforcing Your Mission and Values

What is driving your employees to show up when it's a cold, rainy day? Why does your business exist? What is the big goal of the company? Of course every employee should be financially motivated, but that will often only get you the bare minimum of performance. If you can bring everyone into the mission of the company, you can excite employees to another level of engagement.

In the prior section on product market fit, you picked an exciting industry, found a huge burning problem, and developed an interesting solution to that problem. You can use this to energize your workforce. Today, your mission is to solve that problem. In the future, your vision will go beyond the immediate problem of building a business that shapes your industry.

Principles of Mission and Vision

1. **Set a flexible mission and a big vision:** Evaluate it quarterly; your mission should be built for change.

2. **Pick a focused set of unique core values:** Values should be realistic, not a tool to lure talent.
3. **Reinforce your values throughout your everyday operations:** Reintroduce the core company principles in each department.

Set a Flexible Mission and a Big Vision

As you develop your business to find product market fit, you should also define your mission and vision. Don't worry about picking something that will be carved into the company for all time; your mission and vision will likely change dramatically over time. The important thing is to have some form of mission and vision at any given time that helps align the decisions you make.

For TapCommerce, our mission was to be the global leader in mobile app retargeting. We didn't really have a larger vision that we defined, and that was a factor in why we sold the company relatively early in its history. We were good at carving out a solution niche, but we didn't have a plan for ultimate expansion.

For Attentive, our mission was to be the leader in SMS marketing, and our vision was to reinvent the way businesses and consumers communicate. Over time, we came to evolve that vision to the type of interactions we wanted to empower, so we updated our vision to "create magical conversations." The vision has helped us in assessing our product road map and technology investments; for each we can ask if these investments align with our great vision for the business.

To create the mission for your business, I would simply define the buyer problem and how you are solving it. For vision, I would explain what you would like to be a few years from now. As your business matures and you completely change your buyer problems, solutions, and other elements, feel free to update your mission and vision. Just make sure everyone knows what your business stands for on any given day.

Pick a Focused Set of Unique Core Values

Your company should not be for everyone, and your values should be the reality of working at your company, not a tool to get the most candidates as possible.

At TapCommerce, we never defined the company culture. We had no set of documented values nor a company mission beyond making a successful business. We were a strong team of hardworking grinders, though we were quite inexperienced and short-term focused. Ultimately the business was acquired by Twitter within two years of founding.

At Twitter, we were a big company with a long list of ten core values imprinted throughout the company's training, operations, and decision-making. The company did a great job of reminding the employees of the core values, but the list was too long and often contradictory, leading to lack of clarity of the company's ultimate goals and priorities.

I left Twitter in 2016 to start Franklin (which became Attentive). About two years into the new business, we formally defined our company values and mission. Prior to defined values, our executive team lived and breathed the values together in a small office space, so it didn't feel like it needed definition. When we reached over fifty employees, cracks started to show up. An employee asked about whether to give a dishonest answer to a customer. Another employee was putting projects on very long time lines. We created core values to help employees make decisions in line with our founding team's values without needing feedback on every decision.

In our first pass on defining our values, our management team agreed on eight core values. The values were:

1. Integrity First
Whether internally or externally, let's bring honesty above all to build trust.

2. Default to Action
Because doing nothing is also a choice, and when in doubt, let's act with urgency.

3. Lots of Laughs
Important to have fun and embrace humor to add levity to stressful, high-pace situations. Appreciate each other's company.

4. Listen & Cultivate Discussion
Have opinions, but be willing to listen to ideas and thoughts to change them.

5. Be Attentive
Be polite and courteous.

6. Be Gritty
Be a water carrier and embrace failure and feedback to get better.

7. Use Sugar
Be positive and create an atmosphere where achieving anything is possible.

8. Take Ownership
Be resourceful and relentless to own the project/goal, and run through the finish.

They were all good values, but in retrospect eight was far too many values for most people to remember, and we ended up just focusing on a few that resonated the most with our executive team.

Years later, we more formally amended our values to four core values:

1. Default to action: Speed is our best offense and defense.
2. Hard work solves big problems. Success requires grit and resilience.
3. Never settle: Continuously raise the bar for yourself and your teammates.
4. Be attentive: Work together as a team to drive greatness for our company and our customers.

If someone made me pick just one thing that defines our company more than anything else it would be the first value—default to action. If a company can make decisions quickly, and be willing to change direction, it can be a huge competitive advantage. In the software business, it is often a requirement for long-term competitive success.

I've also found that a value is particularly good if your hiring manager or recruiting team complains about the value because it makes it harder to find candidates. Our value around hard work made it clear that we had high expectations for how much time, and more importantly focus, an employee spent working each day.

To push this point, when hiring the first fifty people, I would often have a "warning" interview to set expectations clearly with the candidate for the role. My warning was that the job was demanding, and if the candidate would rather pursue employment at a much larger tech company, they could make more money (short term) for significantly less work. Our job, on the other hand, offered more learning, faster advancement, and maybe dollar upside through stock equity. My goal was to make sure they did not take the job if they didn't know exactly what they were signing up for. If the candidate took the other job at a large tech company, then our company would not be the right place for them anyways.

Reinforce Your Values Throughout Your Everyday Operations

Values are worthless unless you ruthlessly enforce them across your business operations. Values should be imprinted in the processes of the company. Team members should be able to recount them at a moment's notice. Here are a few examples of ways you can instill your values into your business.

- **Interview questions:** At Attentive, we assess candidates using interview questions to match with our core values. If someone scores poorly against several values, then they are likely not a good fit for the company. The interview process goes both ways. Candidates should also understand the company's values, so they can walk away from the job if it doesn't align with their personal values.

- **Performance reviews and promotions:** When reviewing your team's performance, we ask the managers and peers whether someone is matching the core values against the responsibilities of their role. If they are failing to meet with a value, work to improve it before the next review.
- **Major decisions:** When stuck with a particularly important or unclear decision, go back to your list of core values. If each value got a vote, which way would they go on this decision and why? This can help crystallize hard decision-making.

You should also remind and communicate your values to your team on an ongoing basis. At Attentive, we list the values out at the start of every all hands meeting and board meeting. We inject the values into the templates for one-on-one meetings (see the chapter on How to Build Relationships with a Growing Team). We also include the values in your team emails and even client communications. We list them on our corporate website, in our LinkedIn company page, and in all of our job listings. People should know what the company stands for and what makes it different.

CHAPTER 6
How to Generate Focus and Alignment

The jump from a large business to a startup can be quite jarring. At a large company, your day is pretty regimented. I started my career in sales at CNET.com. After a lengthy training process, I was given a list of prospect accounts, and told to call and email them to set up sales meetings. Each day, I made my way through the list, calling, emailing, and replying to get meetings.

When I moved to a tech startup, that process disappeared. I was simply given a goal—find $100k a month in revenue as fast as possible. A big part of my job was creating a list of priorities, and deciding where to spend time to be successful.

In this chapter, we will go through some of the operations that have helped to make my companies successful. These strategies start at the individual level, with a personal revolving list of top three priorities, and expand to team-wide systems like meeting templates, and review processes. One of the biggest advantages of a startup is its speed. With these processes, my goal is to add structure without creating bureaucracy that can slow the speed of your business.

Principles of Focus and Alignment

1. **Everyone needs a top three:** Each team member should have a list of their top three priorities that they review and update monthly.
2. **Make a weekly executive meeting:** Use the time to celebrate wins, coordinate top three initiatives, and open discussion on important issues.
3. **Set a template agenda for every one-on-one meeting:** It is typically the most common meeting and can be very high leverage if used appropriately.
4. **Conduct rolling 360 ratings, with scores, across your executive team:** Help your team get better, while also understanding the candid views of performance across your team.

Everyone Needs a Top Three

At any given moment in time, there usually aren't that many things that *really* matter in order to make sure your business is successful. Nevertheless, it's very easy to get pulled into working on low-leverage, unimportant tasks. Often these tasks are attractive because: it solves a problem that particularly annoys you, it's something you can do easily without too much thought, or it's simply a more pleasant task to do.

Time is your most precious commodity, and you need to focus your efforts on the most important thing at any given moment. At Attentive, we use a framework called "Top 3 Priorities" which allows our team members to focus on the three most important things they need to do on any given day. Everyone keeps their top three list, and publishes it across the company's executives every month. This ensures everyone knows what everyone else is working on and why. Here is a bit more information on how to set up your own organization top three.

General Top Three Principles

Time allocation: I would recommend that each person should spend at least 70 percent of their working time to make progress on their top three initiatives. This should be true for almost every role. As a test, at the start of the week, a team member can check their calendar to see how many meetings are relevant for their top three or not. If it makes up more than 30 percent of their time, they should consider not attending or deleting the meetings that don't impact their top three.

Helping others: Of course in work we aren't just limited to working on our own top threes, but also in helping others to achieve their top threes. The 30 percent time exists to support other people in achieving their top three, while also doing other everyday work that may be required from a particular role. When requested to do something for somebody else, though, you should ask if it is in their top three or not. If it is not, you should bring this up to them, and there is a good chance it doesn't need to be completed, or that the top three list needs to be calibrated accordingly.

A common issue I've seen a few times is a person who doesn't respect the prioritization and time of everyone else in the company. I had a VP once who published a top three, but in reality would push twenty projects at any given time. While initially this may sound exciting (what a great worker) it is actually really harmful to the company. This person is pushing a lot of initiatives that are not very important and monopolizing the time of other people in order to do their chosen agenda items. By using a top three, we ensure that resources are spread evenly, and individuals who make fast progress will get more slots as they complete one of their items.

Making Your Top Three

I create my top three priorities by making a big list of all the particular projects I could be doing or working on. I then go through the list and order the list from highest priority to lower priority. For each priority, I set a definition of the priority, what I need to do, and the goal I wish to achieve to complete it. For example, it might look something like this:

1. Priority: Operations Leadership Recruiting
Actions: Recruit a new head of operations by completing the job description, posting the job, emailing network for recommendations, writing the questions, reviewing with the team, interviewing candidates, and selecting a candidate to make an offer.
Goal: Hire head of operations by August 1.

2. Priority: Rent New Office Space
Actions: Review potential office locations. Select a winning candidate. Review and sign paperwork. Book movers as needed. Purchase necessary equipment.
Goal: New office move complete by August 1.

3. Priority: Sign a Large New Customer
Actions: Prepare for a large customer meeting. Attend large customer meetings. Send follow-up to customer meetings.
Goal: Sign large customer by August 1.

Other items that didn't make the top three:

- Visit top ten existing clients (leaving to CRO)
- Set up holiday party (outsourcing to firm)
- Meeting with investors (waiting two months)

Once I have my list together, I put it in a shared Google Doc that all of my team can see. In the beginning, this would be everyone in the company. Later on, this might be limited to direct reports or their direct reports accordingly. Additionally, all of these folks also put their top three priorities in the document as well, along with items that didn't make the list.

By putting all of the top threes in one document together, the team is able to:

- Increase awareness of the top three so each team member knows when they may have requests in service of helping the top three initiative.
- Discuss their top threes with the broader team to get feedback if anything is missing, and help on suggestions to fix any particular issue they may be running into.

Outside of Google Docs, we have also tried this process using other project management tools like monday.com and Trello. Ultimately, though, we have gone back to Google Docs because of the ability to easily comment and collaborate in real time, and because our business runs lots of processes in Google Docs. You should live this process in whatever software you find your team best communicates in.

If you make progress on the most important initiatives at the company, you have a much better chance of being successful. Conversely, if you try to keep twenty different balls in the air all the time, you will never make much progress on anything.

Make a Weekly Executive Meeting

At the middle of any high-performing business is a great executive team. Performance comes from great communication and proper prioritization. As such, it's important the executive team makes recurring and significant time to ensure alignment across the team, and open discussion to tackle the meatiest problems.

At Attentive, we have a rolling template we use for executive meetings. We use a shared Google Doc in the meeting, which all members of the meeting have open on a laptop during the meeting. Everyone can write into the Google Doc, and we use the Google Doc as a record of the meeting for future review.

We have the meeting every Monday for about two hours. Here is some of the content we cover in the meetings. Note that this content is what we used at scale with a large team. In the earlier days, I would probably make the meeting even longer, and spend more time drilling into the most important issues in each top three.

Standard Weekly Template:

- **Wins:** This is a list of what went well since the last time you had the meeting. Everyone should open the Google Doc and take a few minutes to list a few things that went well. Once everyone has added a few things, the group can then go through the list together and learn while also celebrating achievements. Sharing in the wins helps the team to bond and keeps a strong morale.
- **Metrics:** If your business is already operating, it's important you are tracking the performance of the business, and that all executive team members understand that performance in regards to the decisions they make. Consider setting one principal person as responsible for gathering the metrics of the business each week. Hopefully you can automate as much as possible to minimize the long-term workload and increase the accessibility of the data.
- **Top three:** As mentioned in the prior section, everyone should have a written version of their personal top three. In the meeting, I recommend each person select one item from their top three they want to discuss with the group to get help and feedback. They could explain the issue they are running into, then provide a place in the Google Doc for people to write responses. One other idea is to ask the group if anyone thinks one of the items from below your top three should have a higher priority and why.

It can also be helpful to change the theme of the meeting each week to spend more time on a certain area of your business operations. At Attentive, we break down the month into the following weekly themes:

- **Week 1:** Metrics and top three
- **Week 2:** Go-to-market issues (marketing, sales, and customer service)
- **Week 3:** Engineering product and design
- **Week 4:** General administration (finance, legal, HR)

Require a Template Agenda for Every One-on-One Meeting

One-on-one meetings are often the most time-consuming meeting for any company. If you look at the calendar for your team, especially as you get larger, you will see a tremendous amount of one-on-one meetings. How do you ensure that all of that time is well spent?

The one-on-one meeting can be a magical way for a manager to coach an employee, help them unblock issues, and solve big meaty topics. Unfortunately, I've seen one-on-one meetings generally waste a tremendous amount of time. The reasons are a lack of agenda for the meeting and lack of preparation. Typical meetings consisted of a manager showing up a few minutes late, the two people chatting about various topics with no fixed agenda, and then a meeting concluded with unclear actions or next steps. In the best-case scenario, you will sometimes see the junior employee prepare a list of items they wish to discuss with their manager in these meetings, but it can be a lot better.

By requiring a templatized agenda for every one-on-one in the company, filled out by the direct report before the meeting, you can ensure that this huge amount of time is not wasted. At Attentive, we made our agenda inspired by some of my executive coaching sessions with Matt Mochary, the best CEO coach on the planet. Here is what we try to cover in every meeting, in order. The actual template is in plain text, and my comments are *in italics.* I've provided below the template, along with a sample version filled out to help explain it.

ATTENTIVE ONE-ON-ONE TEMPLATE

THE GOOD:

- What are some positive things that have happened in your professional or personal life?
- *Comment: It's really important that the direct report fills this out, and that the manager takes time to discuss it during the meeting. Sometimes one-on-ones tend to focus on the problems without recognizing all the great work. By first recognizing the wins and building trust, it will be easier to tackle problems together.*

ISSUE:

- What is the biggest issue you are dealing with now at work?
- What did you do to create this issue? How do you plan to overcome it?
- *Comment: 1-on-1 time is best spent working on the most significant issues the direct report is encountering in their work life, or in some cases, even their personal life. Our*

structure for explaining the issue is to first say what it is, then explain what exactly the direct report did to create the problem. By defining their control over the problem, the direct report can then more clearly understand actions they can take to conquer the issue.

TOP THREE*

- #1: Priority, Tasks, Goal
- #2: Priority, Tasks, Goal
- #3: Priority, Tasks, Goal
- Didn't make list
- *Comment: Standard top three priority list, as described in the section earlier "Everyone Needs a Top Three."*

TOPICS:

- What other topics would you like to discuss?
- *Comment: A list of tactical issues the direct report may have to discuss with their manager in order to get quick feedback or approvals on a particular issue.*

DIRECT REPORT TO MANAGER FEEDBACK:

- Like: What do you *like* that your manager did in this session or since your last one-on-one?
- Wish: What do you *wish* that your manager was doing to help you?
- *Comment: Every meeting should close with an opportunity for each party to get honest feedback from the other party. That feedback is broken down into "Like" positive feedback, and "Wish" constructive critical feedback.*

MANAGER TO DIRECT REPORT FEEDBACK:

- Like: What do you *like* that your direct report did since the last meeting?
- Wish: What do you *wish* that your direct report was doing or had done differently?
- *Comment: The feedback goes both ways. First the direct report gives it to the manager, then the manager can return it to the direct report. This way both sides can be heard.*

Before the meeting, the manager would ask their direct report to prepare for the one-on-one by filling out this template. Here is an example of a prefilled template:

THE GOOD:

- Personal: My daughter did her first weekend of soccer and loved it.
- Work: We beat our annual goals by $5M+ in revenue.
- Work: We just finished a really awesome road map for Q1.

ISSUE:

- Biggest Issue: I am pacing behind my goals for q1 revenue bookings.
- What I did: I didn't generate enough new potential sales deals.
- Solution: Generate more sales deals now.

TOP THREE*

1. **Priority: Operations Leadership Recruiting**
    - **Actions:** Recruit a new head of operations by completing the job description, posting the job,

emailing network for recommendations, writing the questions, reviewing with the team, interviewing candidates, and selecting a candidate to make an offer.
- **Goal:** Hire head of operations by August 1.

2. **Priority: Rent New Office Space**
    - **Actions:** Review potential office locations. Select a winning candidate. Review and sign paperwork. Book movers as needed. Purchase necessary equipment.
    - **Goal:** New office move complete by August 1.

3. **Priority: Sign a Large New Customer**
    - **Actions:** Prepare for a large customer meeting. Attend large customer meetings. Send follow-up to customer meeting.
    - **Goal:** Sign large customer by August 1.

Other items that didn't make the top three:
- Visit top ten existing clients (leaving to CRO)
- Set up holiday party (outsourcing to firm)
- Meeting with investors (waiting two months)

TOPICS:

Review venture capital list
Review office furniture list

DIRECT REPORT TO MANAGER FEEDBACK:

Like: Clear feedback on goals that matter to the company
Wish: Better advice and support on helping with my top issue

MANAGER TO DIRECT REPORT FEEDBACK:

Like: NA—not part of prep

Wish: NA—not part of prep

* Note: Your top three may be excluded from the top three if it already exists in another recurring meeting format across the team. Nevertheless, it can be helpful to repeat it here in this context.

Tactical Details of One-on-One:

- **Tracking:** At Attentive, we run this template through a software called Lattice that also administers our pulse surveys and feedback process. Earlier in the company history, we did it all in Google Docs. Whatever tool you use, I encourage making it easy for people to use it, and checking in occasionally to push people to use this system. If they don't like using the system, listen to their feedback. I've found better managers embrace systems like this to support their team as best they can.
- **Cadence:** How often should you do one-on-ones with this agenda? Minimum is probably monthly, and maximum biweekly. In early usage, biweekly is probably right, then move to monthly over time.
- **Length:** I recommend a minimum of one hour for this meeting. If you find some really meaty problems to dig into, then it can run for ninety minutes up to two hours. If you see your meetings not reaching this length, it may be due to not enough preparation or a lack of trust in sharing and discussing the real issues.

Every company and culture is different, and you will likely want to adapt this template to fit the needs of your team and business. Nevertheless, adapting a template will help get the most out of one-on-one meetings, and if there were three things I would strongly recommend keeping in some form, it would be: Wins, Biggest Issue, Feedback. With these sections, you can build trust, tackle big issues, and get the critical feedback needed to get better.

Conduct Rolling 360 Ratings, with Scores, Across Your Executive Team

As I mentioned earlier in the book, getting honest critical feedback is really hard. At Attentive, we have implemented a 360 rating process that provides both quantitative and qualitative feedback across our executive team. This process has helped me to coach our executive team and also make changes to the team when improvement seemed unlikely. Here is a quick guide to how the process works.

Each quarter, I send a survey around to all of my direct reports. In the survey, I ask them to provide a 1–10 rating for each of their peers, along with feedback on what the person is doing well, and what they wish the person would do differently. The results are visible only to me, so my team is willing to share their candid and critical feedback without fear of retribution.

Using the survey results, I then personally assemble a quarterly performance report for each member of my team. The report includes: Their average performance score from the current period, a reminder of their score from the prior period (to see if they are improving or not), and then highlights on what went well and what needs improvement. When assembling the feedback, I work to remove any information that could be identifying in order to preserve the confidential nature of the feedback. I also work to include the feedback I agree with, and sometimes minimize some of the feedback that I think is unwarranted or less helpful.

Employees who listen to this regular quarterly feedback tend to see a material improvement in their performance output. I've seen employees undergo major transformations and become incredible operators over the course of a few performance cycles. Conversely, some employees will not listen to the feedback, and I've found these folks unfortunately often do not last long in the company, especially as the company grows and their role may require more change.

CHAPTER 7

How to Build Relationships with a Growing Team

In your startup journey, you are going to see high peaks and deep valleys. Trust and friendship among your team makes dealing with the ups and downs a lot easier. Trust allows you to have spirited debates and discussions about decisions and features without getting personal or emotional. Friendship helps you to assume best intentions from each other during times of conflict.

In this chapter, we will review some strategies you can deploy to build trust and friendship among your team. These are predominantly simple things, but also things I have found it can be easy to overlook, including regular lunches and personalized onboarding. Finally, you can see fantastic leverage by spending the time to deliver a great all-hands meeting to your team.

Principles of Relationship Building

1. **Set up a regular one-on-one lunch program with your team:** Spend time outside the office to learn more information, solve problems, and build relationships.

2. **Build relationships through digital personal connections:** Use some tips and tricks to quickly make connections with your expanding team.
3. **Create a regular all-hands:** Focus on transparent information sharing delivered with an element of entertainment and fun.

Set Up a Regular One-on-One Lunch Program with Your Team

Going to lunch with teammates has always been one of my favorite things about work. One issue, though, is you can go into a cycle of always going to lunch with the same few people and miss a big opportunity to listen to different viewpoints.

It sounds very simple, but consider committing to a regular lunch meeting with a rotating set of people on your team. Sometimes the lunch can be one-on-one, and in other contexts it can be across an entire team. I've found that when you go to a less formal context, and just get chatting, some of the most creative thinking and solutions can flourish.

If your company does in-office catering, I recommend leaving the office for these lunches anyways. The additional aspect of going to a restaurant helps create additional space for building a relationship and also maybe sparking creative ideas.

Build Relationships through Personalized Onboarding

During Attentive's company onboarding, we ask each new employee to take a survey about themselves. This survey includes information like:

- Favorite candy
- Favorite movie/book/art
- Ultimate professional dream
- Goals in the next few years
- Other personal and professional questions

This information is shared across the team, and can be used to deliver a personalized onboarding experience to the employee. For example, we can do simple stuff like mail them some of their favorite candy. More importantly, we can understand the employee's professional goals, and check how we are doing on achieving them at the three- and six-month employment markers.

Create a Regular All-Hands

To create a community, you need to bring everyone together, optimally in person, on a regular basis. You want them engaged, excited, and open to learning and sharing more about themselves, their roles, and the company. At some businesses, the all-hands meeting is very formal and quite boring. At a startup, it's easy to make all-hands meetings authentic and fun. You can make it something most people look forward to and almost everyone attends.

At Attentive, we hosted an in-person all-hands. We did it monthly for the first few years of the company. When COVID-19 hit, we switched it to remote, and moved it to weekly in order to reinforce the community while remote. All-hands was primarily hosted by me (the CEO), along with our head of recruiting Sean McDermott, who moonlighted as a stand-up comedian. I strongly recommend having several cohosts to liven up the meeting and open room for humor and freshness.

We cut a variety of different segments for our all-hands, so here is a quick run-through of how we did it, and I hope this helps you when putting together your all-hands:

Format

- Hosted on Zoom as well as in person
- The tone was similar to a late-night talk show. We actually had a stage with talk show desks and chairs when we did it in person.
- Music was played for the start, ending, and sound effects went off at planned times during the show.
- Length was typically one hour long
- Timing was on Thursday afternoons around 5 p.m., sometimes Fridays

Content

- **Business performance review:** We shared metrics similar to those mentioned in the sections in this book on board management and product market fit. After board meetings, I presented the actual board deck, removing any particularly personal or sensitive information but keeping 95 percent of the content.
- **New team members:** We introduced new team members, and often had a game-show format for them in which they would compete in a fun quiz game.
- **Department-level updates:** Teams with a particular win or achievement would present that to the company. These presentations were typically led by the

individual most responsible, not necessarily the leader of the department.

- **Attentive All Stars:** We sent out a form where people could nominate other employees for an employee of the month award called "Attentive All Stars." The winners would then find out during the meeting. Whoever nominated them gave the speech to introduce them, then the winner gave a quick acceptance speech. Prizes ranged from medium-sized to extravagant. I liked the more extreme prizes like a trip to Italy or a large appliance.
- **Questions:** The CEO answered questions brought up in a survey sent before the meeting. We didn't answer questions live but rather only prescreened questions to make sure we gave correct and thoughtful answers.
- **Other entertainment:** We also hired entertainers from time to time to spice up the show. This included people like mimes, ventriloquists, comedians, magicians, singers, and all sorts of fun folks.
- **Talent show:** We asked employees to present talents to the group.
- **Seasonal items:** We ran a variety of seasonal content like a Halloween-costume dog and cat parade, holiday-oriented costumes, and themed guest hosts.

The all-hands meeting was integral to building the Attentive community. It helped to bring the company values into company-wide communication, and also helped to create a connection between leadership teams and the distributed workforce. Please consider setting up an entertaining and information-packed all-hands that your team likes to attend. Supplement your all-hands by also writing a weekly or monthly thoughtful email to the team that reinforces all-hands content, but also reaches everyone across the company in case they couldn't make all-hands.

CHAPTER 8

Building the Ideal Work Environment

Building a successful startup is really hard. You have a lot of work to do in understanding the changing marketplace, designing and adapting solutions, and winning against the competition. You will spend a lot of time together, whether at an office, over lunches, on videoconference calls or at off-site locations. Be deliberate to create environments that maximize the impact of these settings.

In this chapter, we will review some of our most successful practices for creating a productive work environment. This includes options for setting up your offices, perks and benefits that impact productivity, and opportunities to build relationships and trust like offsites.

Principles of the Work Environment

1. **Spend time together in an office:** Get faster execution and enhanced collaboration through a shared physical workspace.

2. **Design a working environment to maximize collaboration and output:** Foster an environment for creative thinking and quick actions.
3. **Free lunch and free snacks are a great investment for an in-person team:** Develop opportunities for team building while also saving mental time for everyone.

Spend Time Together in an Office

At Attentive, we worked in one office in New York for the first three years of the company and built a deep culture. Once COVID-19 hit, we went fully remote, but we were able to take some of the deep culture we had built and scale it to our remote teams. Once the world started to reopen, we opened an office in New York and San Francisco, and encouraged in-person events, while also allowing most roles to work remotely. For my executive team, we have set up a monthly three-day in-person off-site, in which we deep dive into the most important issues of the company. This has proven to be really effective for us, hitting the right cadence of time to get together in person.

So what's the right recipe for remote work? Every business is different, but I think there needs to be some component of work together in an office, even if for a few days each month, and it's especially critical in the early days of a company where you are building your trust and relationships. Some of the appeals of getting together in person include:

Fun

Part of the appeal of working for an early-stage startup is to have fun at work. Let's face it—working remotely isn't always the most fun. You spend more time with your family, and you don't spend time commuting, but it can be monotonous and boring to stare at a screen all day and eat a sandwich. One of the best things about working in a startup is spending your time around great people working on a big problem together.

At Attentive, we had a vibrant culture of ongoing fun. Our team didn't have big salaries, but we would splurge on great takeout food, regular sit-down lunches, and of course the requisite happy hour. Six years later, our team still reminisces about some of our best outings and the great fun we had. We also built friendships to last a lifetime, which gets to my next point.

Relationships, Trust, and Issue Resolution

It is much easier to build relationships in person than it is to build them remotely. At Attentive, during the first few years of the company, we went to *a lot* of lunches. You can go to lunch with someone one time and call them a friend, but join ten Zoom calls together and still not think of them as a friend.

Friendships and relationships matter deeply when dealing with the various issues that come up with growing and managing a company. Over the course of my companies, I have gotten into frequent arguments and disagreements with cofounders and early employees. You get mad, maybe even yell a bit, but then you cool down. You can come back to your friendship or relationship to resolve it quickly. It all comes back to a mutual sense of trust and respect for each other that allows easy issue resolution. These relationships are so much harder to build remotely, and thus much harder to manage through.

Issue Creation

How many times do you get into an argument with someone over Slack or email? It is easy for that to happen because feedback and criticism always comes off much sharper when presented in the written word.

When Attentive went remote during COVID-19, we noticed a significant uptick in petty issues driving major personnel problems. A common complaint was, "That person is a jerk." When I would ask a follow-up question on why they were a jerk, it was often something the person said or did in Slack or an email.

A Zoom call or a phone call can be a better way to deal with issues, but even then it's often missing critical information about body language, setting, and other cues that are hard to make out without being in person. Simply by being in person, interpersonal issues often immediately disappear.

Design a Working Environment to Maximize Collaboration and Output

Getting a little more tactical, if you have decided to work in person, let's review some best practices for how to ensure you are creating the best possible in-person work environment.

Coworking Spaces

You may think you have a good plan on the usage of your office space, but I've broken every lease I have signed. At Attentive, we started in a sublease of a small literary office. We ended up raising some money sooner than expected and moved out just four months into our one-year lease. We signed our second office for a two-year term, and we stayed for about one year total. We signed our third office for a three-year term, and we ended up expanding significantly into two neighboring spaces and then terminating it during COVID-19. Finally, we signed a large new space for three years, didn't use it enough, canceled it, and signed a new lease for one year. So, take my advice: You will likely change your office space a bit to fit your needs.

Finding and signing an office lease can be a huge investment. Most of our companies started in the days before widespread usage of WeWork and similar coworking spaces, so we didn't have much experience with them in our HQ, but did spin up WeWork for all of our remote offices. If I was starting a business today, I would almost certainly sublease a small office within a WeWork or similar coworking space or sublease until we had more than fifteen people.

After surpassing fifteen employees, when I had raised enough capital for more than eighteen months of runway, I would lease an office for the shortest time period possible, optimally a year. This flexibility is essential as it allows you to lease a space that is only big enough to accommodate a year of growth, and also doesn't make you responsible for something much bigger.

When doing the lease, make sure you spend the money to have appropriate real estate counsel review the paperwork. You don't need to redline it like crazy, like most of my lawyers wanted to do, but you should understand key issues like: How much is the real monthly cost, what happens if we want to break the lease, and who is responsible for payment if the company defaults on lease payment.

Desk Design

Open floor plans have become extremely hot over the last twenty years, and in fairness all of the companies I have started have had open floor plans. If I started a new company today, though, it would be a combination of open plans, cubicles, and many small offices. Different roles need different levels of collaboration, so think about your own organization and what type of setup each department wants.

Think about how you can help your team to be the most effective in however you design the desk space. We bought everyone their own Bose QuietComfort headphones to wear at the office if they'd like to, so that they could focus on their work with no external noise distractions. Personally, even when at home, I often work with a pair of Bose wireless headphones listening to the sounds of rainstorms.

Conference Rooms and Phone Booths

Think carefully about the space requirements for your business, and augment your office space to meet the needs of your team. Personally, I love lots of small meeting rooms and phone booths. Our teams love to quickly huddle in a one-on-one or three- or four-person meeting, so we made meeting rooms that size. As work has gone remote, even if you go into an office, you will inevitably find more and more people dialing in remotely. You need more space to fit this change.

At Attentive, we bought phone booth meeting rooms from a variety of companies. In the early days, we were really cheap and I searched Craigslist for "phone booths," "isolation rooms," and "recording rooms." We found two rooms locally for around $1k each, and went out in a truck, bought them for cash, and brought them back to the office. It took us an hour or two to cut off all the excess glue and assemble them, but they worked really well. Later on, we bought professional phone booth rooms from a company called Room.com.

Engineering, Design, and Product Room

Engineering, Design, and Product (EDP) are really hard jobs that require intense focus and close collaboration. At Attentive, we created an EDP conference room where the EDP team sat and worked together. The room was mostly quiet with team members wearing their own noise-canceling headphones. The room was equipped with several rolling whiteboards, a nice view of the outdoors, a lot of snacks, and even a dedicated fridge. If you want the team to work a lot together in a relatively small space, then build a place where they feel comfortable to stay for a while.

Free Lunch and Free Snacks Are a Great Investment for an In-Person Team

Have you ever spent 20–30 minutes looking through online menus deciding what you want, or going through Yelp to pick the place to go? Once you decide, it can take a long time to go to the venue, get the food, meet the delivery person, deal with lateness and other issues etc., and it might not be with your coworkers. If someone fails to get food, they can become quite hangry (hunger-related anger), which I've seen derail many a midday to afternoon meeting.

A totally free, catered lunch is a big investment, but it can produce phenomenal returns. You can save a tremendous amount of your team's time, while also creating an opportunity to build trust and culture.

When I think about what I miss the most working remotely, it's eating lunch with my friends at work. Lunch is a great time to relax, step away from work, and chat with your coworkers. Sometimes you might talk about work-related matters, other times you might just talk about life and day-to-day issues. In both cases, it's a great opportunity to learn about each other and build a relationship around friendship and trust.

It's a similar idea with snacks, drinks, and caffeine. Rather than making people take a big disruption to their day, you can encourage break time as a chance to build relationships with coworkers. You want to make it easy for your team to have what they need so they can focus their time on work, or on building trust and relationships with their coworkers.

Part 3
Team

Once you have found a problem in a market you are passionate about, building your team is the most important factor in determining the success of your company. Beyond business success, you are picking the people that you will spend a tremendous amount of time with over the next several years, and sometimes even decades. You can always change your business strategies, but it's much harder to change the people on your team, especially as your business gets older and your team owns part of the business.

A great team is the output of a lot of really hard work. Teams do not self-assemble. Behind each team is a talent builder who works tirelessly to assemble great people, set an audacious mission, and help them to all work together.

In this section, we will cover some of the nuts and bolts of building a stellar team of people. We will start by looking closely at what type of team you want to build, then dig into strategies for making a talent funnel and closing great talent. We will cover how to get into the startup talent ecosystem, review sample interviews, and cover various tips and tricks for building your all-star team.

CHAPTER 9

Defining the Team You Want to Build

You have defined your core business problem, evolved a unique product solution, and taken your first pass of cultural values. It's time to build a team that you love spending time with, and that will support each other through the highs and especially the lows of a startup.

In this chapter, we will explore what makes a great team member and stress the importance of shooting for fantastic people in your first ten team members. Then we will expand that by mapping all of the roles you will need in your initial team recipe to deliver a successful solution.

Principles of Team Definition

1. **Find Builders:** People who love to work and want to make something great.
2. **Write an ideal team recipe:** Map your business to the market needs and write interview questions to match those skill sets.
3. **Set a very high bar for your first ten employees:** Your early team has an exponential impact.

Find Builders

So what type of people do you want on your team?

Above all other traits, I love to hire builders for early-stage startup companies. Builders are people who love to make things. They like to work hard, get their hands really dirty, and aren't afraid to take ownership and get something going. They want to do things themselves rather than rely on assigning and delegating to a team. These builders are often not successful at large established companies, but they are critical to getting off the ground today.

I often find builders have big ambitions they want to achieve, and some initial pride and ownership over prior accomplishments. So how can you identify builders in an interview? Here are some questions I've found useful to find builders:

Q: What is your dream job and why?
Commentary: Builders often have big ambitions. I love to hear they want to start their own businesses. They are on the right career path for their dreams.

Q: What is your greatest accomplishment?
Commentary: Personal and professional, but I like the initial question to be open ended. What do they value so far? Are they happy with it or do they want more?

Q: Can you think of something you built of which you are proud? (It can be a physical thing or an intangible thing, and encourage it to be nonprofessional.) Follow-up: Explain to me the process you took to build it.
Commentary: Some people can seem to be builders but when you dig in they really are just explaining someone

else's project. If you ask follow-up questions you can understand how intimately they were involved in building the project.

Q: What would you like to build at our startup?

Commentary: I wanna see excitement to jump in and take ownership here.

Some other traits I've also found to be essential in builder mindsets include coachability, curiosity, and being hardworking. Here are some questions to consider using to judge these traits.

Q (Coachability): How would you rate your performance in this interview so far on a 1–10 scale? [Answer]. Follow-up: Why do you feel that way? Follow-up: What would you do to improve your score next time?

Commentary: Most coachable people will provide a lower score, and then provide some thoughtful ways to improve. They recognize their prior issues, and think of ways to do better in the future.

Q (Curiosity): What is a recent book you have read? What is your favorite book? What magazines or websites do you read regularly and why? What sort of things do you do for fun or other interests?

Commentary: I've seen a high overlap with people who enjoy reading and general curiosity/intelligence. Also, I find a quick assessment of their reading and leisure helps me understand what the person values.

Q (Hard Working): What does your ideal working day look like and why? What do you enjoy the most about work?

Commentary: There is a decent chunk of the population that likes to work, and it's mostly because they have found something they are interested in. If the person truly loves to work in your area, then they will describe a day packed with work as the most exciting. Startup life is demanding and stressful. They need to understand that going in.

Now that we have defined some high-level attributes for potential team members, with a focus on builders, let's examine what the best possible team composition looks like.

Write an Ideal Team Recipe

Every business has different needs for their core starting team. For most businesses, though, I would simplify the team equation to two components: product and sales. You need someone to make the product, and you need someone to sell it.

For these components, write out all the different projects and tasks you envision this role will be responsible for. Use this list to create your interview questions for potential candidates and score them on their abilities to deliver these goals.

Within your first ten team members, you should have someone who is great in each of these areas. Optimally, you should also avoid duplication of skills within your cofounding or executive team, and instead seek teammates with complementary skill sets.

Set a Very High Bar for Your First Ten Employees

The first ten employees will have a tremendous impact on the business. The first ten will recruit the next forty employees, set the cultural norms, and make key decisions that make or break the company.

Finding your first team is very hard. Startups require employees to provide a ton of additional work for significantly less money in the short to medium term, with the dream of maybe a financial reward in the distant future. Employees need to be driven by their love for the challenge, and the potential to make a real impact each day. They need to like working.

When I started TapCommerce, I had trouble finding a great team, because I didn't know how to recruit great talent. Taking a startup job is a big risk, and I was an unproven entrepreneur. Almost everyone said no. We ended up building a successful company, but our team was relatively inexperienced and unbalanced. Our team was very junior, and thus we tended to hire even less experienced people.

When I started my second company, Attentive, I understood how to build a talent funnel, as highlighted in the next chapter. I was able to recruit from a much wider network with a higher success rate. Our first ten employees were incredible, and as a result they hired fantastic teams.

CHAPTER 10

Building Your Talent Funnel

In the early days of a startup, it's probably the CEO along with a couple of cofounders. Everyone is likely working for nothing but equity and living off savings. For my first startup, I remember having saved about $50k in my bank account to live on until we could find a way to pay ourselves. For the first few months, we hired a couple of interns to help, but couldn't pay any full-time salaries until we raised venture capital.

Whatever your situation, hiring full-time, paid employees is a big step for any startup and a major commitment not to be taken lightly. To be ready to hire full-time paid employees, you need money to pay them, a clear customer problem to solve, and a defined solution to build and sell. If you can check all of these boxes, then you are ready to consider adding people to your team.

In this chapter, we will go through some of the popular ways to drive talent to your company, so you can build a big pipeline of great people. We will get a bit tactical, and go through some of the ways you can engage potential employees through various communication channels to drum up interest.

And finally, a reminder of persistence: Most people are very hard to reach, especially for your first unproven startup, so don't get rattled. Keep trying!

Principles of the Talent Funnel

1. **Spend 50 percent of your time recruiting:** The more time you spend, the better the quality of your team.
2. **Manually build talent flow with cold messages:** Use social and other channels to personally connect with potential team members.
3. **Most people don't reply to the first email or message:** Don't get discouraged; be relentless.

Spend 50 Percent of Your Time Developing Talent Pipelines

As we mentioned in the last chapter, the first ten employees will have a tremendous impact on the business. The first ten will recruit the next forty employees, set the cultural norms, and make key decisions that make or break the company.

When you are hiring your first ten people, consider spending half or more of your time focused on recruiting to develop a talent pipeline. Every CEO will tell you that they spend a lot of their time recruiting, but if you actually look at the calendar, I've found it is often less than 25 percent of my time. There are a ton of people out there looking to work in startups and build great businesses, but they can be hard to reach. You need to develop a pipeline of different sources of talent to maximize the amount of applicants into your future business. Consider some of these ways to build your startup network:

In a Startup Job

There is a certain type of person who thirsts to work at a small company and have a big impact. People who already work at a startup are much more likely to consider joining your startup. If you haven't already worked at a startup, and you are struggling to build your own team, then you should go get a startup job and build your network. You can build great relationships with coworkers and the community that may later turn into startup cofounders. Here are a few examples.

- **Workplace events:** Ask coworkers to lunches, dinners, and drinks. When I had my first job at a startup internet company, I tried to go to lunch almost every day with a lot of different people from the company. When I went to start my own company years later, I hired some of those people as early team members.
- **Trips:** Set up a trip with colleagues. Traveling together is an amazing way to build a deeper bond much faster.
- **Sports/special events:** Create a company sporting team, or way to get together regularly with hobbies that creates camaraderie.
- **Ask questions:** Ask people about their hopes, dreams, and goals. You can learn about them to help them achieve their goals, and they will want to work with you to do so. This also helps understand quickly who shares your interests and who may not.
- **Conferences/meetups:** Go to every meetup and conference opportunity you find in your interest area.

School

On my first day of business school, I recruited the CTO for my first company. At the day one welcome party, I told anyone that would listen that I worked in tech startups and was looking for cofounders to start tech companies. Of the entire class of a few hundred people, there were a handful of people who were interested in tech startups. More specifically, there were less than six who were interested in tech startups and also had some software engineering capabilities. I had lengthy conversations with two of them, and it ultimately came down to commitment. The first guy was leaning more toward investment banking, the second guy was willing to go all in on startups.

Investors

Early-stage investors, often referred to as "seed" investors, meet a lot of people in startups, especially the type of cofounders you are looking for. As a result, if you email them and say you are looking to get introduced to smart cofounders, they may be able to help you. They are motivated by helping the companies they are already invested in, but they are also motivated by future investments, and they love the idea of putting a team together. Overall, emailing them can be a bit of a long shot, but if you can attend their various meetups and happy hours, you could find some more like-minded people. This will also be important when it comes to fundraising, which we will dig deep into in a later chapter.

To create a list of seed and early-stage investors, go to this book's part on fundraising, and jump to the chapter on how to get venture capital meetings. This includes information on building a list of relevant investors in your local area to build your community.

Manually Build Talent Flow with Cold Messages

Warm networks (like former coworkers, schools, friends) are an excellent source of hires as they tend to have a significantly higher rate of turning into employees than cold channels. Unfortunately, warm networks also typically run out of candidates pretty quickly. When you have exhausted all of your warm sources for team member leads, it's time to start building your hiring funnel with cold outreach. Cold outreach will be the core of most of your hiring. So remember the quote, "A stranger is a friend you haven't met."

About half of TapCommerce's first twenty employees came through completely cold outreach. For Attentive, fourteen of the first twenty hires came through completely cold outreach. You may find this surprising given the network of talent available for a serial entrepreneur, but the reality was that we needed to hire a lot of entry-level to relatively junior roles, and to reach those candidates we had to go outside our network of more experienced operators. Here's what we did to drive those candidates:

#1 Create a List of Target Companies and Roles

Begin your cold outreach by creating a list of all of the people you want to target for the roles. For each role, there are two key dimensions to understand: target companies and adjacent roles.

For companies, you should make a list of all the companies from which you wish to recruit talent. For Attentive, this list included all of the large software providers in our geographic area, along with all of the medium to smaller businesses in our industry landscape. To find the businesses, try searching for industry maps. Often investors publish lists or graphics showcasing all of the businesses in a given industry. For instance, the investment bank LUMA Partners publishes a "LUMAScape"[4] that includes all of the business names and categories for a particular industry.

For roles, for each of the jobs you are hiring, put together a list of all of the prior or current roles a potential candidate should have experience in. For example, if you are hiring a salesperson, you could be looking for someone that has been an "account executive" or an "account manager."

#2 Use a Job Search Engine to Create a Candidate List

Open a job search engine website and input your search criteria for companies and roles to create a list of potential candidates. The best system today is LinkedIn Recruiter/Navigator, which allows you to simply copy and paste your list of target companies and roles to create a list of potential candidates. Go through the candidate lists and filter the results to create a saved group of potential targets by role. You can do this by going through each person individually and assessing whether their profile of skills and experience appears to be a fit for your role. When in doubt, cast a wide

4 Lumapartners.com/lumascapes/.

net because you want to create as much volume into your job funnel as possible.

#3 Send Messages

Use a job search engine, like LinkedIn, to send individual candidate messages. These messages perform a lot better if they are sent directly from the CEO/founder of the company rather than a member of your recruiting or HR team. Here are some examples of the real messages I sent from Attentive to reach our early team members:

> Subject: Lead role, message from CEO, sold prior co to Twitter
> *Hi* [Name],
>
> [Personalized first sentence based on their experience]
>
> *Any interest in joining a hot new startup with a significant equity package, strong base salary, and proven technical team?*
>
> *Our team sold our last company to Twitter and now we have a new one called Attentive. Any interest in joining the core tech team?*
>
> *Learn more:* [Link to job description]
>
> *Cheers,*
> *Brian*

Depending on the type of roles targeted, this message along with several follow-up messages would get a 10–30 percent reply rate, quickly building a funnel of high-quality candidates to interview.

Most People Don't Reply to the First Email or Message

Don't be upset if you don't get a reply to your first email or LinkedIn message. Almost no one replies to the first email or message. Oftentimes it will take several emails, LinkedIn messages, and social media notes until the recipient responds. They will be impressed by your perseverance, as they may know this is a critical trait for startup success. Most people give up with one email.

CHAPTER 11
How to Manage the Interview Process

You recognize the importance of building an amazing team, so you have put the work in to build a big pipeline of great talent to work at your company. You have an exciting big problem to solve, a well-packaged mission and vision, and a distinct culture to attract the best talent. You need to protect these massive investments by running a seamless and engaging candidate interview process.

In this chapter, we will run through the tactical steps to running a tight recruiting process for an early-stage startup. We will explore the steps to construct the optimal interview process in detail and ensure you can quickly act on hires as a significant competitive advantage. Hiring is one of if not the most important thing you will do, so it's important the CEO and founders stay extremely close to each hire and do everything possible to land the best candidates.

Principles of the Interview Process

1. **Use a shared doc with detailed custom questions for each role:** Ensure answers are clearly tracked and scored in the doc or an applicant tracking system.

2. **Make a hiring committee for every role:** Create an aggregate candidate score, and require at least one champion per hire.
3. **Move fast:** Your greatest advantage in hiring is your speed.
4. **Stay involved in closing every hire:** For mid- to senior-level hires, C-level selling is a big advantage.
5. **Hire a head of recruiting early:** Maximize your hiring pipeline and deliver an exceptional candidate experience.

Use a Shared Doc with Detailed Custom Questions for Each Role

Some companies create one standard list of questions and proceed to ask it for almost every role. The reality is that even in early-stage companies there is a lot of specialization, and this demands a more customized approach to interview assessments. Instead of one common list of questions, I recommend you take the time to create a custom set of interview questions for every role that match the skills and qualifications for the role. It will take you more time to come up with these questions, but it will allow you to better score the qualifications of each candidate.

Start the process by creating a shared Google spreadsheet and make a column list of all of the skills and attributes required for the role. Next, create another column and write a corresponding interview question for each of these skills and attributes. For every interview conducted, simply fill out a column with the answers provided by the candidates. As your company scales, you may consider using an applicant tracking system (ATS) that has tools for inputting these types of questions and forms. Nevertheless, even now I still use Google Sheets for easy manipulation and comparison. I find it easier to digest and play with the data than to do everything in a more rigid ATS system.

At Attentive, account managers are responsible for the relationship between the company and the customer. We created a list of attributes for account managers, then mapped them to interview questions accordingly. Below is a list of some of the attributes we set for a first or second interview, and the questions we asked related to that attribute.

Customer Success Experience	
ATTRIBUTE	**QUESTION**
General Job Experience	
Account Experience	How many accounts do you manage in your role today? What kind of accounts are they?
Skills/Efficiency	What are the essential tools and favorite tools to integrate for sales operations?
Process	What sort of process do you have set up for managing accounts today? How do you follow that process?
Analytics	How do you track the success of your account management?
Learning/Curiosity	What have you done in the last year to learn more about account management?
Cutting Edge	What is something you have done in account management that you think shows you are on the cutting edge or innovative in account management?
Work Ethic	
Pushing Bar	What is a project that you completed in your current job that would not have happened without you?

Challenge	What was the biggest challenge you encountered on the job—how did you deal with it?
Results	What sort of results do you typically like to track yourself on? What do you think the OKRs are for Account Management?
Time and Availability	What sort of typical schedule do you operate on? Mornings or nights? Other issues? What time requirements do you have?
Drive/Reason	
Why Startups	Why do you want to work at a technology startup?
Why Attentive	Why do you want to work at Attentive?
1-Year Goal	Where would you like to be in 1 year?
3-Year Goal	Where would you like to be in 3 Years?
10-Year Goal	Where would you like to be in 10 years?
Why Leave?	Why are you leaving your current job?
Why Account Management?	Why do you like to work in account management?
Important Behaviors	
Motivation	What motivates you to work as hard as you do?
Persistence	Describe a recent example of when you went the extra mile to get a renewal.
Time Management	How do you manage your time? What do you do to stay organized?

Make a Hiring Committee for Every Role

For each role you hire, you should have the candidate interview with the same group of people on your team. This group is called the hiring committee. Early in the life of your company, this means every candidate could interview with all of your cofounders or early senior team members. Later on, the candidate may only meet a small subset of the company that is more directly aligned with the role they will be playing on the team.

To run the candidate through the hiring committee, we would divide the questions assembled in the prior section across the panel of people who will interview the person, and also create some repetition in the questions for particularly important skills. Interviews would record the applicant's response, and then also score each response on a 1–10 scale. At the end of the interview, we used the responses to calculate an average score for the applicants' performance against our attributes. Through interviewing many candidates for a role, we could calibrate the scores, figure out which applicants scored at the top, and progress those applicants to additional interviews, and ultimately a job offer.

After a candidate completes the interview process, the committee should meet to review the candidates' results and make a decision on the candidate. During this process, I like the idea of requiring a champion. Someone on the hiring committee needs to speak out personally to *champion* the hiring of the candidate. This means the champion on the committee is confident in the success of the candidate, and will help them to ramp up in their new role. If the candidate does great in the role, then the champion is recognized for their support. Conversely, if the candidate is not successful then the champion is also accountable for this failure. If a candidate can't find a champion, then it's likely not someone the company should hire.

Move Fast: Speed Is Your Greatest Advantage

As with many things in life, whoever makes the first offer usually ends up getting the deal. As a result, to win in the hiring process you need to move extremely quickly to reach the best candidates. Big companies will likely have larger cash offers and more impressive brand names, but they move slowly. You can beat them with your speed.

Collapse the steps in the hiring process to fit into the smallest time window possible. Optimally the entire hiring process can fit in a two- or three-day period. Here is how we structured the process at Attentive:

- The first day includes a phone screen of the candidate.
- The second day includes an in-person interview with the hiring committee.
- The third day includes references and an offer to the candidate.

To fit such a tight time line, you need to be constantly pushing to the next step in the process. If a phone screen goes well, then schedule their in-person interview on the call. If the in-person goes well, then request references and review salary needs before the candidate leaves the office. Call, text, and email references immediately and repeatedly until you get the answers you need to proceed.

When it comes time to give an offer, make a generous first offer to entice the best talent. If you have a good amount of cash, then offer a market base salary and equity. If you don't have enough cash for a market salary, then you will need to be really generous with equity.

It is tempting to try to keep the offer as low as possible. The problem is that a low accepted offer will often introduce trouble in the short to medium term. I have "won" a negotiation landing at a relatively low salary, only for a candidate to leave the company because they subsequently received a much higher offer. Remember, candidates are talking to many employers, and great talent is going to get a lot of offers.

Ultimately, you want your team to be very excited to be working at your company. You will demand a lot of passion and hard work from your team, especially at the early stages, so everyone should receive a great compensation they are excited about.

Stay Involved in Closing Every Hire

It can be tempting to leave the closing of candidates to the hiring manager, or someone in your recruiting team. For the first fifty hires, when every great hire has tremendous leverage, I recommend the CEO take the additional time to do follow-up calls with the candidate and get the person to say yes. Similar to speed, access to the CEO is a unique value proposition that other larger, more established companies will not offer. It also highlights for the candidate the extreme level of access they will have in their new job regularly interacting with the management team.

At Attentive and TapCommerce, I would call candidates without a scheduled time to chat, as this helped to create an air of excitement to the call. I found it was especially effective to ask a candidate to explain their objections that may be standing in the way of accepting the job offer. Sometimes very small changes in the offer letter or compensation can lead to a quick acceptance, so be straightforward and ask the candidate anything that could be stopping them from saying yes to the job today.

In addition to calls from the CEO, the chief revenue officer (CRO) of Attentive came up with an exciting video package we now prepare for new senior hires. Using a website called tribute.co, we assemble small videos across the entire team that interviewed the candidate sharing their excitement about the candidate joining the team, along with a quick description of some of the issues we hope to tackle together. These types of videos create a special and personal experience for the candidate and have had a very high success rate.

Hire a Head of Recruiting Early

As you no doubt understand from all of the steps described in this chapter, recruiting is an extremely demanding, full-time job. Moreover, the more time you put into the job of recruiting, the more candidates you will drive into your hiring funnels, and thus the better the quality of your hires and your team.

In my last two companies, I have added a full-time head of recruitment within the first twenty employees. Although this is considered early for a recruiting hire, in each case, I wish I had done it even sooner. I was lucky to partner with Sean McDermott, the best recruiter in tech startups, who taught me a lot of the process and tactics to find top talent.

When done right at scale, the recruiting team is a seamless extension of the hiring manager and C-level executives of your company. Recruiting helps build a massive funnel of candidates while also fostering a great candidate experience, an extremely fast process, and ultimately a high hit rate of success in hiring great team members.

Part 4
Marketing

No one cares about your product. They care about their problems and what you are doing to solve those problems. Great marketing captures buyers with a burning customer problem, and then magically weaves in their solution.

Creating urgency is at the center of all marketing and sales. Buyers have a lot of things to do in their life. They are busy. They have a lot of distractions and other priorities. You need buyers to feel the need to act now. If not, they may be pulled into another problem, or even worse, another solution.

In this section, we will help establish some initial marketing goals, review marketing fundamentals, and push to help customers to feel that urgency to act. Once you have goals set, we will focus on different strategies for reaching your buyer to drive sales, then consider some applications post-sale to drive retention and continuous growth. The best marketing performance is driven by a continuous evolution of testing new strategies, tweaks to improve existing programs, and relentless focus on driving results.

CHAPTER 12
Basic Marketing Setup and Goal Setting

In building your business, you have identified a real customer problem, built a great solution, and hired an incredible team to take your product to the world. Now you are ready to take your creation to the masses. But how do you reach them?

In this chapter, we will cover some of the marketing basics to get your business off the ground, then set some ambitious goals to scale fast. This begins with tactical items like your initial company name and product name, and how to hire and compensate marketing members to focus on hitting these goals.

Principles of Marketing Basics

1. **Evolve your company and product name:** Keep flexibility to enable evolution and nimble changes to your business.
2. **Sell the problem:** Not your solution.
3. **Pay marketing like salespeople**: Align your team's compensation with your desired outputs.

4. **The goal is category leadership.** The top business in an industry will attract better talent and drive outsize performance.

Evolve Your Company and Product Name

Founding teams spend way too much time agonizing over the name of their company. I suggest a two-step process—incorporation name and product name.

1. Incorporation Name:

First, incorporate with a generic name. You may have seen some companies do this. Pick a street name you grew up on, or a general hobby or interest, and add labs to the end.

Examples:

Crestview Labs Inc.: Street name where you grew up Labs
Surfwax Media Inc.: A fun activity you like Media
Yellow Notepad Project Inc.: The stuff on your desk Project

Okay, now you have a name for your overall holding company, and complete flexibility over your future product and business name.

2. Product/Business Name

Now you need a name for your initial product. Recognize that you might change it, but just something, anything, will do for the first pass. I think the more the name aligns with what the initial product does, the better results in experimentation.

Remember, you aren't going to post about this on social media or put it out there anywhere yet (hopefully), so who cares about the company name. Yes, you will need it to recruit people so it does need to have some name, but don't agonize over it. Personally, I like posting the job listings as a "stealth startup" in the early days more than actually listing the company name. The type of employee you want at the earliest stage will be excited by getting in so early that the company is secretive or doesn't even have a formal name.

Here is a quick list of some things to consider:

- Buy a .com name, but with an additional word added to your product name if needed. For Attentive, we just owned AttentiveMobile.com for 6 years until we finally bought Attentive.com. You could also buy a domain with a .io or .ai or some other ending. Dot com, though, can create more immediate legitimacy and trust with both consumers and businesses, so I buy it whenever financially feasible.
- Grab some social media names, but do it using a new Gmail account. You should buy your business social name on Twitter, Instagram, TikTok, etc. . . . but again don't link to your email, or some friends and family may find it and start asking you about it.
- Once you are seeing some success, have your lawyers do a quick trademark search on the name. You want to make sure that there isn't a very similar company with the trademark name that could block you just as you

are starting to build some brand equity. But generally that can come later.

Remember that almost every successful tech company has changed their name once, if not several times, through the life of their business. Google's original name was "backrub," and it recently changed its overall name to Alphabet. Facebook was originally "theFacebook" and is now called Meta. Your name is going to change over time, so don't get wedded to one particular one.

Sell the Problem (Not Your Solution)

Buyers don't care about your solution. They care about their own problems, and want ways to solve their problems. Earlier in the "Product Market Fit" part of this book, we talked about the importance of finding the buyer's problem. Early marketing and sales is all about experimenting with different ways to reach and find the buyer's problem.

When reaching out to prospective customers, you need to lead with the customer's potential problems. If they are open to hearing more from you, then you know you have the right problems. If after talking to you, they want to try your solution, then you may have the right solution too.

When we first started selling Attentive, we took the wrong approach and got very little interest. Our first sales email messages were focused on the solution. We wrote emails to customers with subject lines like "Interested in SMS Marketing for YourBrand" and "SMS marketing reaches 90%+ open rates."

When we changed to focusing on the problem, we saw much better results. Our initial buyer was someone who worked in marketing at an ecommerce-focused retail brand. Our customer's problem was that they needed to find ways to grow their revenue significantly every year. Their entire job was to find another 20–50 percent in growth every year.

As a result, we started sending emails with subject lines like "20% more revenue, free trial" and "Make [custom estimate] for [brand name]." In the second example, as provided in the section on "making a great email preview," we customized the message with a first-year revenue estimate based on the company's web traffic, and also included their brand name.

Instead of ignoring our emails, brands now began to take real interest and respond. In many cases, they didn't believe we could have this type of impact on their business (we could), but they were open to listening because we were solving their customer problem—revenue.

Pay Marketing Like Salespeople

At a lot of companies, you will see a marketing hire get a flat base compensation, but a salesperson making significant dollar-based commissions. Instead, I would suggest playing with marketing compensation to align with sales-based compensation.

Pay your marketing team in line with the output you desire. At Attentive, we paid marketing for the amount of conversations they drove between Attentive and potential customers. Our marketing team had the opportunity to make a lot of additional cash if they drove a lot of meetings with potential customers. As a result, they worked really hard to hit and exceed that number each quarter.

The Goal Is Category Leadership

Look at the top most valued companies in the world today.

1. Apple—mobile phones/pcs
2. Microsoft—operating system/business software
3. Saudi Aramco—oil
4. Google—search
5. Amazon—ecommerce
6. Berkshire Hathaway—various
7. Nvidia—chips
8. Tesla—electric cars
9. Meta—social media
10. J&J—consumer packaged goods

Almost every company here is a category leader. Consumers and businesses usually want to buy the well-known and trustworthy brand to avoid risk. People are going to buy the category leader. Due to this dynamic, category leaders are often able to charge higher prices, make greater margins, and have lower churn rates. As a result, investors tend to give the category leaders big premiums in terms of price and long-term potential.

For category leadership, you have two options: create an entirely new category, or pick a category with weak leadership in a dynamic market. For my companies, we have done both.

For TapCommerce, we solved the problem of low mobile app retention rates with app retargeting. After a consumer downloads a mobile app (such as eBay or Angry Birds), only 5 percent of consumers are still using that app six months after installing it. When we started TapCommerce, retargeting was common on laptops and desktops, but had not yet been successful on smartphone mobile apps. There were one or two companies experimenting with the strategy, but it wasn't their core business.

We started Attentive in 2016, when text messaging was well over twenty years old. I recall one of our investors even told me the story that he had personally sold a text message marketing business over fifteen years *before* the founding of our company. So clearly we were not creating an entirely new type of category—well, not yet anyway.

There were a half dozen or so text message marketing companies operating at decent scale throughout the United States, and they all seemed to be ashamed of their core business. If you went to one of their websites, it was hard to know what they actually did. They spent most of their marketing materials trying to push ancillary products related to whatever was the new in-vogue software area—customer data platforms, mobile wallets, or mobile app notifications.

What we realized, though, was that text messaging was an amazing communication channel that was completely underused due to a lack of providers offering great text messaging software. With the advent of smartphones with mobile applications, software vendors had turned their focus toward mobile app software, but consumers still loved text messaging. Simply put, text messaging wasn't cool, but it was ubiquitous and incredibly effective. We built solutions to make text messaging great.

CHAPTER 13
Reaching Your Buyer

You have already put together the most basic components of your marketing strategy. You picked a name for your company and your products, hired a marketing team motivated to drive results, and set some ambitious goals to own your industry. Now let's get into the tactical instruction on delivering marketing success for your business.

In this chapter, we will dig into essential tactics to ensure you can reach your buyer. This begins with the core messaging of your product, what is front and center on your website, physical locations, or physical marketing materials. We will encourage you to repeat this communication many times, as it can be hard to break through the noise and reach your buyer. Finally, we will break out a few examples of how to gain momentum with your buyers in the process of turning your business into a category leader.

Principles of Reaching Your Buyer

1. **Say what the company does in clear language:** Don't get pulled into overly creative language that confuses potential customers.

2. **Embrace repetition:** Most people aren't paying attention or reading each line closely.
3. **Aggressively fund better and better case studies:** Move toward bigger brands and more engaging stories.
4. **Use company events for great content:** Combine in-person sales with scalable solutions to grow your brand presence.

Say What the Company Does in Clear Language

How often do you go to a company website and you can't figure out what the company actually does? This happens a lot in enterprise software, and it is greatly damaging to the company. I also see it infect itself into the sales deck, the pitch deck, and other collateral. You can have a twenty- or thirty-minute meeting and come out of it saying, "So what does this company actually do?"

Marketers are inherently creative people, and come up with great ways to position their business and brand. Unfortunately, this creativity can also do a lot of damage when it comes to communicating your company's solution to your buyer, especially early in your life.

There are two basic ways to explain what your company does: the problem you are solving and the solution you provide. To ensure you avoid marketing buzzwords, you should explain both problem and solution in the simplest words possible. Show your copy to a few people who are not involved in your industry, and make sure they can understand it. Early on, if your product category is still being defined, you may start with the problem and end with the solution. Later, you may find you are leading with the solution, then introducing the problem.

When we started marketing Attentive's product, very few businesses wanted to buy text message marketing tools in our industry. Our website said, "Discover a way to drive 20% more revenue . . . using Text Message Marketing." We are leading with the problem, and then beginning to introduce the solution. Today in 2022, text message marketing is now very popular with our customers, so we use our headline to simply state what we do, then follow with the problem. "Attentive: The most comprehensive text message marketing solution. Attentive will make SMS your next top 3 revenue channel."

When in doubt, you should lead with your problem, and then succinctly explain your solution in basic words. Avoid marketing jargon or internal language.

Embrace Repetition

Back in one of my early companies, I was meeting with a potential customer, selling an advertising product called "CommentSurf." Our product would show advertisements next to the comments section of an article on a website, with ads that looked like comments. After about fifteen minutes pitching, the buyer asked, "Why would I want you to write articles for my website?" The buyer did not understand what our business did even after fifteen minutes. It is easy to get frustrated by these situations, but they happen all the time.

As entrepreneurs, we live and breathe our product every day. As a result, it is easy to lose touch with what life is like for our buyer who may only have an extremely limited exposure to our business. The buyer may have back-to-back meetings and ten other things going on in a given day. They need your product and pitch to be simplified. At the core of that simplicity is repetition of your core problem and solution.

According to the National Association of Sales Professionals, "Repetition is the key to sales success."[5] Most people who visit your website will quickly scan one or two pages. If you want to get your message across, you must constantly repeat yourself—on your website, in your sales deck, and throughout your marketing materials.

If something is really important, make sure you say it three times at a minimum. The worst case scenario of repetition is that the potential customer says, "Okay, I get it," which is a great response. The bad scenario is the buyer misses critical information about your problem or solution, and doesn't understand what you do.

Aggressively Fund Better and Better Case Studies

Most B2B companies start by selling their product to small and medium-size customers, then graduate to larger and larger customers over time. The faster a B2B company can move to larger customers, the more dollars they will find. Generally larger businesses spend significantly more than smaller companies but cost a similar amount to acquire.

Once you have a working product, marketing should make it one of their top three priorities to create a progression

---

5 Ingham, Gavin. "Repetition Is the Key to Sales Success." *Influencers Invited* (blog). nasp.com/blog/repetition-is-the-key-to-sales-success/.

of case studies toward larger and larger customers. When you launch your first customers, they will likely be smaller companies, and that's a great place to make a case study. You can then use those case studies to sign bigger and bigger customers, and in turn, get case studies from these bigger, better-known businesses.

Consider aggressive strategies in order to get case studies developed as soon as possible. Here are some of the tactics we used at Attentive:

- Include significant discounts or credits for case studies as part of the customer onboarding. This includes agreeing on when a customer will be happy to provide a case study, with the shortest time window possible.
- Provide cash-based or equity-based bonuses, to your marketing and sales team members who are able to get case studies made that meet your specifications.
- Pay more (internally and externally) for well-known brands, or larger business case studies.
- Develop relationships with the points of contact with the companies that are providing the case studies. It is very likely that prospective customers and, if things go well, prospective investors, will contact these people.

Use Company Events for Great Content

We went to market with Attentive in May 2017 and launched our first customers in June and July 2017. By the end of the summer, we had half a dozen happy customers, and we were adding a handful of customers each month. Against that backdrop, we decided to do a courageous thing—we hosted our first customer conference in September 2017. It had a tremendous impact on our business.

Let's face it, when you are early in your life as a company, it is really hard to get customers to pay attention to you. Sales needs all the help they can get to entice a prospect to consider using your product. Dedicated customer conferences allow your business to reach your customers in three important ways: an excuse to email and invite, meeting prospects, and content creation for legitimacy.

At Attentive, we started by making a splash page (still live at https://messageone.splashthat.com/) to the event that showcased an impressive-looking venue, along with the logos of speakers and attendees. The page you see is the final version, but the earliest version had no logos. We invited every friend or significant other from reputable companies we could find to assemble meaningful logo lists of attendees. We then continuously updated the website as we got better attendees, and also incorporated those logos and information in our email signatures and invites to prospects.

In the run-up to the event, we used this to continuously invite customers as an excuse to try to get a demo, and also to highlight the "industry trend" around text message marketing. Many customers couldn't make the conference, but they did pay attention to the trend, and as a result set up a meeting or booked one in the future.

At the event, we focused on having sales conversations, but we worked even harder to get content. We hired a videographer to record our customers giving quick testimonials at a step-and-repeat wall, and got professional pictures of the speakers at the venue. A lot of the speakers were either very early customers or industry friends, but the end output was an impressive-looking display of a company that was growing.

We used this content all over our marketing materials. We put it on the front page of our website—showing quotes from the conference, cleaned-up videos, and key takeaways. We put it into white papers that our team sent out to a lot of prospects. And we added it to the front of our sales deck to highlight how big of a trend this was in the industry.

The results were astounding. When we launched our event, we were signing up two or three customers a month. After the event, we started consistently signing over ten customers a month. Before the event, when we spoke to a potential customer, they were never familiar with Attentive. After the event, some prospects reported some familiarity with our business. The event allowed another way to reach potential customers without directly pitching them.

Part 5
Sales and Customer Service

For startup companies, proper sales execution is often the difference between success and failure. The first twenty or thirty customers can make or break a business. A great early member of the sales team can make your business work. In my companies, I've been very lucky to work with exceptional sales teams that helped get us off the ground, and I personally participated in most of the sales for our first fifty or more customers.

When I was graduating from college, I knew I wanted to eventually start a tech company, but I wasn't sure the best path to get there. I didn't have money or a big idea, but I was willing to work hard and learn. Most of my friends steered me in the direction of prestigious jobs in consulting and finance with the theory that I would learn a ton in these roles. I just wasn't excited to work on consulting projects for big companies making often-unused PowerPoint presentations.

One of my most successful family friends, though, strongly encouraged me to pursue a job in sales, working at a medium-sized tech company. He explained that sales was at the center of any company, meeting customers and delivering the product. If you do sales, you can understand how the business actually works and get into the technology world.

I've seen many founders reluctant to get involved in sales. They are hesitant to meet and sell to customers, and instead hire salespeople to meet with their customers. A founder will work tirelessly on building a product for months, sometimes even years, before they go sell it to a customer. As you may guess, this usually leads to failure.

Founders need to talk to customers now, and the first step is getting comfortable with being a salesperson for your business. My sales experience has been the biggest reason for my success, and I encourage all entrepreneurs to jump into sales and learn how to work with their customers. Moreover, sales is a critical skill that you can use throughout your professional and personal life. You need strong sales skills to recruit talent to your business, raise venture funding, and forge partnerships with other businesses.

In this section, we will dig deeply into the details of running a great sales process. We will cover how to hire your sales team, how to get meetings with potential customers, and how to pitch and close those customers. We will also look at how to measure your sales performance over time in order to adjust your strategies and improve. Finally, we will also look at some best practices for managing customers and upselling.

CHAPTER 14
Sales Is a Critical Product Research Tool

You have built a real product that solves a burning problem for customers. You are assembling a team of driven builders to help put your business on the map. You have a thoughtful marketing strategy that reaches your customer with clear language explaining the buyer's problem and your solution. Now you want to start driving some sales, so you are pushing to hire salespeople.

A lot of the professional world still looks down at sales as replaceable and unintelligent. As a result, I still see a lot of companies that show little respect to their sales team and quickly dismiss their thoughts and feedback. These companies are missing out on a huge opportunity to listen to their customers, and also potentially dooming their business.

In this chapter, we will encourage you to hire salespeople early and often to help you learn from your customers. Sales is the key to business growth, but it can also be an incredible way to shape your products and services based on listening to your customers. We will explain some of the best ways we've found great salespeople, and help you to grab your first batch of recruits.

Principles of Sales Product Research

1. **Hire salespeople in your founding team; it's an investment in your product:** Great sales engagements will lead to a deeper understanding about the customer problem.
2. **Recruit fresh inside salespeople with some experience:** Ensure they have what is needed to hit the ground running without a burned-out view of meeting generation.
3. **Pay sales cash for every meeting:** Compensate individuals to align with the job they are responsible for delivering to ensure continued engagement and excitement.

Hire Salespeople in Your Founding Team; It's an Investment in Your Product

As soon as possible in your company's history, you should hire inside salespeople (often called SDRs, or sales development representatives) to experiment with selling your product. I have seen *so many* startup founders resist hiring salespeople, particularly inside salespeople, that I must take considerable effort explaining why it's *so* important to hire salespeople *extremely* early on.

An inside salesperson is someone whose primary job is setting up meetings with potential customer prospects. They are called inside because they stay in the office and do not generally go to meet customers in person. They are typically a couple of years of experience to entry-level sales roles. If they are successful in setting up a meeting, they will then hand off the meeting to an "outside salesperson" who will do a meeting with the potential customer in person or over the phone. Outside salespeople can be very expensive and more challenging to hire. Inside salespeople are much less expensive, and much cheaper than every other role in the company including engineers or product managers. You can typically hire three inside salespeople for the cost of maybe one engineer.

At Attentive, we hired four inside salespeople in our first ten employees, and it had a huge positive impact on the company's trajectory. With four inside salespeople, we were able to populate a rich database of prospects. From that database, we were able to set up about twenty meetings per week, or about five per inside salesperson. As a result, we pitched a lot of customers and got a lot of customer feedback early, along with a very healthy sales funnel. This allowed us to pivot our product quickly, and to grow sales fast.

Here are some of the common objections I have heard to why someone hasn't hired inside salespeople, and here are my responses:

"We aren't ready to sell yet."

As mentioned in the chapter on Problem Hunting, you want to set up meetings with potential buyers before you actually build your product. While you can certainly do this without an inside sales team, by having some inside salespeople you will be able to set up a lot more meetings, and get more information.

"I can get my own meetings."

Getting a high volume of quality customer meetings is very time consuming. It's true that founders can get meetings on their own, and if you absolutely don't have money to hire inside salespeople, you may have to get your own meetings for some time period, but it will be at the cost of not making headway on lots of other important things and slow you down considerably. Furthermore, sales is hard, and inside sales is a special skill. Someone you hire will likely do it a lot better than you can at significantly lower cost.

Founders are also likely to take costly shortcuts when booking early sales meetings. They may ping friends or investors for introductions, which can lead to "friendly" meetings that don't deliver the right type of critical feedback—see the chapter on Problem Hunting.

"I hired an intern."

Okay, that's a start, but an intern is not a trained inside salesperson. They will not be able to develop a large number of inside sales meetings for you, but can certainly help the process of expediting your sales team. Consider having the intern help support your inside sales team.

"Maybe I'll just get one inside salesperson."

There are a bunch of good reasons not to hire just one salesperson:

- **False signal:** There is a risk your salesperson is not good. You really won't know if a market is a fit or not with just one salesperson because you will be questioning whether something is wrong with the salesperson when things go poorly.

- **Comradery and competition:** Sales can be a tedious and challenging job where you make hundreds of phone calls without much success. Your team will be a lot more successful if they are surrounded by other people doing the same thing. People they can talk to, learn from, have fun with, and tackle the day together.
- **Burnout and failure:** Many companies experience upward of 50 percent of their inside sales team burning out of the role in less than six months. If you only hire one person, you could find yourself with no inside sales function in a matter of months, especially if they are operating solo. By having numerous people, you can ensure you will always have a stable of inside salespeople to go out and sell.

Recruit Fresh Inside Salespeople with Some Experience

So hopefully by now you have been convinced to hire some inside salespeople. That's great! So how do you find and hire good ones? I'm happy you asked.

For Attentive, we set up a LinkedIn Recruiter account, and we reached out to inside salespeople with the title "sales development representatives" (SDRs) who worked at established startups—companies with hundreds of employees. Our story was that by moving to a newer, smaller company, the SDRs would be able to move up faster, make more money, and get direct experience with the executive team. It was likely more risky than their current role, but also had potentially more upside.

We focused on SDRs who had been in the role for anywhere from a few months up to a year. We wanted people who had been properly trained on how to do the SDR job, but that also hadn't been doing the job too long. Proper training ensured that they would be able to join Attentive and immediately begin booking demos and selling. We avoided people who had been an SDR for a long time at a prior employer to ensure that the person would still be happy to do the SDR job, and would not have expectations of immediate advancement to an account executive selling role.

For our interviews, we asked questions based on what we thought was most important for the SDR roles. We set a list of characteristics we looked for in a hire—coachability, ability to listen, work ethic, etc.—and then judged candidates based on their response. One of our favorite recurring questions series was:

- Curiosity: What is your favorite book?
- Answer: There isn't a right answer here, but just proof that the person is curious and thoughtful.
- Salesmanship/listening: Can you pitch me that book?
- Answer: The best answer is probably a candidate who responds and asks the interviewer, "Well what type of books do you like to read? Have you read this book before? Have you heard of it?" That's a great way to take the conversation, because then the pitch can be personalized.
- Coachability: How did you do on your pitch, with a 1–10 rating?
- Answer: Any answer here less than an 8 is good. Your hope is that the candidate understands that there is always room to get better, and they will be highly receptive to feedback and ways to improve. When

asked to pitch something off the cuff to someone you don't know, no one should be able to do a perfect pitch the first time. It will require improvement.

- Retrospection: Why do you feel that way?
- Answer: Get some more meaning behind the score. Often I have seen candidates lower their score when they think about it a bit more, so it offers a chance for a candidate who quickly gave a high score to show a bit more coachability and introspection.
- Improvement: What would you change next time?
- Answer: Thoughtful analysis of the first pitch and potential changes to the future pitches is always an incredible thing to hear here. You can really see how the candidate thinks.

For each of these questions, we scored their response on a 1–10 scale. Whoever scored the highest received follow-up conversations and ultimately the job. In Q1 of 2017, for Attentive, we interviewed about twenty-five people, and hired four SDRs in our first class. One of the SDRs is still with us as an account executive running a really important function at Attentive (and scored the highest in the interview process), one left and started a company that has raised tens of millions in financing, the third left the sales business, and the fourth left after a few months.

Pay Sales Cash for Every Meeting

Sales is hard work, and early sales can be especially tricky and demotivating. Make sure that your sales team is incentivized to produce the results you want. It's very easy to lose momentum when selling, and you need to keep the team's spirits high as you navigate the business through the trials and tribulations of finding product market fit.

In the early stages of the business, inside salespeople should be paid an additional cash bonus for setting up meetings with prospective customers. They should be paid this bonus regardless of the success of the meeting. For example, you might be willing to pay the inside salesperson anywhere from $100 to $500 for a meeting with a prospective customer. You should also offer additional compensation if the meeting converts into being a customer, as this will ensure that the SDR is booking the right type of meetings, and rewarding the quality of the meeting.

CHAPTER 15

How to Get Meetings with Buyers

Earlier in the "Product Market Fit" section of this book, we explained how to build a list of target buyers, interview potential customers, and refine your problem statement to reach a burning problem. From that work, you defined a burning customer problem, built a tested product solution, and put together a marketing plan to take your product to the world.

In this chapter, we will get into more of the tactical details on how to succeed in getting meetings with your potential buyers. This chapter is focused on B2B (business-to-business) sales, but most of the concepts could also be applied to targeting individual consumer buyers. We will start with building an updated list of target buyers based on an ideal customer profile (ICP), craft an email template to send to buyers, review other channel strategies like phone calls, and finally review some best practice tactics to optimize performance.

Principles of Booking Sales Meetings

1. **Creating a list of target buyers:** Spend the time to ensure you are filling the funnel with the right type of customers and contacts.
2. **Making a great email preview:** Buyers should understand the problem you are solving before opening the email.
3. **Cold calling for voicemails and other aggressive tactics:** Use every possible channel to reach your buyer.
4. **Never say "I want . . ."** It's about what the customer wants.

Creating a List of Target Buyers

The first step in getting a sales meeting is creating a list of potential target customers. You can start by writing up an ideal customer profile (ICP) to define what type of customers you want. For B2B businesses, this includes information on the industry, the size of the company, the location of the business, and the role/title of the people you want to target. For consumer businesses, this could include the age, location, gender, income, and other information about the consumer. For example of a B2B ICP, here was the initial ICP for Attentive:

Example Ideal Customer Profile: Attentive SMS Marketing

Industry: eCommerce, businesses that sell products online as their primary business

Commentary: We chose to start with ecommerce businesses because they are mostly small and nimble companies that are constantly trying out new solutions. They also have a very fast feedback loop, so they can tell you quickly if your product is working. Finally there are a lot of these types of businesses, so it's a big market and therefore easier to find someone willing to try it out.

Location: United States. Optimally New York City (where we were founded)

Commentary: Usually it is easier to start in your local market. This allows you to meet the potential customer in person, learn more from usage, and service anything that may require you to be onsite.

Size: Small to medium size (0–50 employees)

Commentary: Most B2B businesses aspire to sell to medium to large businesses because larger businesses spend a lot more money. Typically, though, it is hard to start your business selling to large businesses because they can take a long time to make decisions, and they also usually do not experiment as much with new solutions. As such, companies usually start by targeting smaller customers, then over time they sell to bigger businesses. This is called "moving upmarket."

Role/Title: CEO, CMO, VP of Marketing

Commentary: To sell your product, you need to reach the decision-maker for the purchase. Targeting C-level executives is called "top-down" selling. You sell first to the top of the organization structure, then it moves down the organization to implementation. This is my preferred way to sell, but it's hard to get meetings and time with executives, so it can be difficult. Inversely, you can also sell to more junior employees, but they will need to get executive approval to proceed. They are easier to get meetings with, but often don't have the authority to proceed and therefore the sales process can be long with a high failure rate. This is called "bottoms-up" sales.

Once you have created your own ICP, you can start building a target list of consumers or companies to sell your product. For consumer sales, you probably can input your target customers into advertising tools like Google Ads or Meta Ads to begin finding your consumers. For B2B sales, you can use tools like ZoomInfo, Seamless.AI, Lusha, and many more. These tools can provide company names, and some solutions also provide the names of potential customers by title. LinkedIn Sales Navigator provides another great way to create lists of contacts for outreach.

Now that you have a list, it's time to start reaching out to customers.

Make a Great Email Preview

Over the years, I've gotten a lot of draft emails sent to me—from sales to marketing to client strategy. In every case, the most important part of the email is the subject line. People sometimes spend so much time on writing the content of the email, but then quickly write the subject line as an afterthought. That's a big mistake.

Stop for a second and consider what the email will look like in the inbox of the buyer. It will show the sender, the subject line, and maybe the first eight to ten words of the message content. This is your chance to get the buyer to read your email. Only a very small percentage of emails are actually going to get read; I probably read less than 5 percent of the emails I receive. You have to make your subject line count and resonate with your buyer.

You can judge the success of your emails by using tracking and automation software like Outreach and Salesloft. This software allows you to test many different types of emails and track analytics like open, click, and response rate. You can refine your concepts over time and see which is resonating with your buyer.

I recommend experimentation with different subject lines to find the best one for your problem. The problem of the business should be in the subject line, but you may be experimenting with many different customer problems. And within each problem, there may be certain elements of the problem that are most compelling. Different lures work on different fish; you need to experiment and try many different angles to get different types of responses.

Once you have a great subject line, spend a lot of time experimenting with the first couple of sentences of the email. I suggest skipping the pleasantries and getting straight to the point—why is this worth the buyer's time? You don't need to start your email with "I hope you are having a nice day," or something like that—just jump right into why you are reaching out.

The best opening is going to explain more about the problem and why you think that problem matters to them, then quickly transition into your solution. In entirety, the email should be short and sweet, so it's easy for the potential buyer to understand the content.

Close your email with a clear call to action. Ask a brief and simple question. Are you open to a meeting? You can use software tools like Chili Piper and Calendly to make scheduling easy, or provide available times. Any step to make it extra easy for the buyer to say yes.

Here is a sample of a successful sales email we created early in the life of Attentive:

> Subject Line: Make $24M in incremental revenue for [Brand], free trial
> Content:
> Hi [Name],
> We estimate you can drive $24M in incremental digital revenue over the next 12 months with Attentive's text message marketing platform. Here is a detailed forecast: [insert link]
>
> Leading ecommerce & retail brands, such as [brand] and [brand], are seeing huge success using Attentive.
>
> We offer a completely free trial to prove it—open to a brief call to learn how other cosmetics brands leverage Attentive?
>
> Cheers,
> [your name]

This email got a very high response rate, so let's analyze a few of the strategies happening in this note. First, the subject line is personalized to the buyer with a customized revenue forecast. At Attentive, we used a system of estimating potential revenue by categorizing the brand's estimated web traffic (using a tool called SimilarWeb). We could then use this data to provide a detailed revenue forecast for the brand. Over time, we also added other brands that used Attentive as a reference in the email. Finally, we push toward a call for a free trial, making it very easy to try out our solution.

Not every buyer is going to respond to the same angle, and you need to try out numerous different hooks to find the right fit. If this email didn't work, we would send numerous follow-up emails. Some emails would have similar content, other emails would be completely different. We would talk about other related issues like the overall decrease in email performance in the market, a specific strategy done by competitors, or recent industry reports. We would often have more than ten touch points into a customer before they agreed to the meeting. So please don't get upset if it takes several notes to be noticed. That is normal.

Cold Calling for Voicemails and Other Aggressive Tactics

Cold calling can be a daunting task. I remember my first experience with cold calling. My manager gave me a big printed list of companies, contacts, and phone numbers, and told me to go down the list. Most people didn't pick up, and if they did, they hung up relatively quickly. A few times a day, though, I got a bite that ultimately led to a meeting. In my first couple of months, I managed to sell a handful of customers, including one customer who went on to sign a massive contract. You want to reach a potential customer any way you can, and some customers are more likely to respond to a phone call or voicemail. As a result, our team at Attentive still uses cold phone calls as part of our standard sales process, and it consistently produces new customers.

Today, most people don't pick up the phone, but almost everyone reads their visual voicemail on their iPhone or at least checks the beginning of audio voicemails. As such, a cold call can be a simple reminder to check your email and see something there. I like to approach voicemail similar to how I would approach an email subject line. After that, I just direct the person to take action by searching their email for my messages. For instance, I might start a voicemail saying, "Do you know your [insert competitor name] saw 20 percent revenue growth using SMS? Search for Attentive in your email to set up a free trial. The email is from Brian Long."

On the unlikely chance the person picks up the phone, I go straight to the buyer problem. "Hi [name], Thanks for picking up. Your competitor is seeing 20 percent annual revenue growth using SMS marketing. Any reason you haven't tried it?" Now of course this is missing an intro to me, but I like to get straight into it, and not give them time to hang up. If this is relevant to them, they will probably ask "Who is this?" and then they will answer the question. I will apologize for not fully introducing myself, go to my pitch, and work to get a demo booked.

Never Say "I Want . . ."

This is a very small note, but it's extremely important to keep in mind when you are composing your emails, or writing a script for cold calls. The conversation is about the customer's problem, and how you can solve it. It is not about what you want.

I still see a ton of salespeople who start emails or conversations with "**I want** to talk to you about X today." "**I want** to share important information with you about Y." Try to eliminate the phrase "**I want**" from your sales vocabulary, and you will see significantly higher response rates. It is hard to eliminate this from your vocabulary—I still make the mistake—but doing so will lead to more sales.

CHAPTER 16

How to Build a Sales Pitch

You've scored a meeting with a major potential customer. They seem to have the core burning problem you identified, and you are excited to explain your solution. The reality of sales, though, is that it can be really hard to get a buyer to take action. You need to tell a bold and entertaining story that drives engagement and urgency from your buyer.

In this chapter, we will review the essential ingredients to a successful sales pitch. If you are creating a B2B company, your sales pitch is the single most important external document you will create. If you make it well, it will lead to adding lots of customers, and thus lots of revenue to fuel future growth and success. If your pitch is not good, then you will fail to sell your product, and your business can fail.

First, we will go through the building blocks of the pitches we have built at my companies. Then we will jump into mechanisms to get continuous feedback and review how to adapt your pitch for better results. Finally, we will focus on identifying the biggest sources of friction to help improve your product and sales strategies.

Principles of Making the Sales Pitch

1. **Tell your story with a clear five-part structure:** Discuss the buyer problem, dig into your solution, and seamlessly transition to how to purchase.
2. **Heavily incentivize buyer feedback:** Reward customers for honest and thoughtful feedback on your product and positioning.
3. **Listen to feedback and constantly change your pitch:** Adapt your approach to the changing market and needs of your buyer.
4. **Remove every source of friction:** Time, risk, and money are often the biggest barriers.

Tell Your Story with a Clear Five-Part Structure

Earlier in the book in the part on Product Market fit, we had a section called "Turn Your SSD into a Pitch," where we broke down an initial pitch for your solution. Your actual sales pitch is the natural evolution of this presentation. There are many things you can choose to add to a sales presentation, but I see the core building blocks being: discover questions, elevator pitch, problem, solution, and a transition to next steps.

For my software companies, usually discovery questions are done without a presentation, and the rest can be done with a mix between a presentation and a live demonstration. I generally prefer a presentation as it allows more information, reduces risk, and is easier to teach to new salespeople. Different businesses, though, may benefit more from demonstrations of their product or service, especially if it's a particularly impressive demonstration.

Discovery Questions

A sales call starts with discovery. Discovery is learning about your customer and why they took the call. Depending on the size of the customer and the typical sales process, sometimes an initial call will be almost entirely discovery and limited information about your company's product and feedback.

For Attentive, we typically spend about 25 to 50 percent of the first sales call on discovery, asking questions to understand the customer's current problem situation. By understanding the customer's current state, you can significantly customize the information you present to make it the most relevant to them, and also increase the likelihood of success. For instance, if a customer is already sold on the need to buy a solution like yours, then you can spend less time on the problem section (below) and more time explaining your product. If a customer is particularly focused on a certain concern, you can spend time addressing that in the product section of your presentation. In an optimal situation, the discovery questions will lead logically into the presentation, as described below.

Elevator Pitch

Once you start presenting, you have a very limited window to keep the attention and interest of the buyer. You don't want the buyer to feel like they are "sitting through a sales presentation" or dealing with someone who is just "reading off a script." It's important to get right into the elevator pitch. In two or three slides, and less than two minutes, you should be able to explain the customer problem, your solution, and why the buyer should give you the time of day.

Personally, I am a big fan of adding in a "sit-up slide" at the end of the elevator pitch. This slide is meant to ensure the buyer is paying attention by making the strongest, boldest claim you can make to address their core problem.

At Attentive, we would provide a forecast on the amount of revenue we could drive for their business. This number was often quite large. The buyer might respond loudly and emotionally saying they don't believe you can provide such a solution. This response is great. You now know they are engaged in the conversation, and they are willing to learn how you can possibly make this solution a reality for them.

Problem

As we discussed in earlier sections, your product is all about solving the buyer's problem. The first section of the deck is about agreeing with the buyer about what their problem is. I like to use this section to show industry trends and in-house surveys which detail the problem we are solving. I will often pause to see if the buyer has feedback, and at the end of the conversation, I will check in with the buyer to see if they have experienced these trends as well. With a positive response, I will confirm they have the problem that our product solves, and now I am ready to jump into our solution.

Solution

If the buyer agrees with your problem, then demonstrating your solution is simply connecting your product to the problems you already identified. This section is the most likely section where you might confuse the buyer. You love your product (or potential product), and you probably have way too many slides, and too much technical detail. Go through your slides and cut half of the product slides. Cut half of the text and ensure each slide has no more than twenty words on it in a maximum of three bullet points. Each slide should only convey one core idea. As your product becomes more complicated you will find yourself adding more and more slides, and that's fine. For your initial product, keep it simple.

Next Steps

If your solution fits the buyer's problem, then it's time to implement it. The final section of the pitch focuses on what steps the buyer needs to take in order to get started. This section lays out the list of things needed to start using the product, and is a perfect segue to closing questions. If the buyer is engaged, you can now ask closing questions. Would you be interested in trying it? What would hold you back from trying a product like this?

Listen to Feedback and Constantly Change Your Pitch

Your pitch and your product should both be constantly changing, and hopefully getting better. By listening to the customer feedback, you can edit each of the sections of your pitch to ensure your pitch aligns with the problem of your buyer, and that your product is solving that problem.

In the early days of my companies, we would constantly change the pitch on almost a daily basis based on customer feedback. When you are small and young, changing the pitch is easy. Very few people are using the pitch materials, and it's easy to learn a few more lines or change around the script based on the feedback you are getting.

As our companies got larger, we changed the pitch less frequently—every month or two for smaller changes, annually for bigger changes. When you have a large salesforce, there is a tremendous amount of training that goes into adjusting the sales presentation. Furthermore, changing the pitch can be risky and create lower win rates on deals while also confusing both salespeople and buyers. Small companies can be nimble and change quickly which offers a big advantage in a world where the buyer's problem can also change fast.

Remove Every Source of Friction

A lot of people think the primary reason someone doesn't buy is the cost. While money is an important dimension, in my experience, there are three main drivers of friction in a sales process: risk, time, and money. You need to study your buyer to understand what is stopping them from saying yes and buying your solution. Deeply understand every objection, along with anything that is slowing down your process. Build products or processes to remove that friction, and you will have a significantly better business. These differences may be the difference between success and failure.

Limiting Risk

For Attentive, we predominantly sell to buyers at medium to large businesses, which we will call "enterprise buyers." Risk is the largest source of friction. Enterprise buyers usually choose to buy the solution that will not get them fired. They work at a big company with likely slow processes and complicated implementations. Buying a new product that takes a lot of resources and time but doesn't show results can get them in a lot of trouble and lead to being fired. On the other hand, maintaining the status quo is usually a successful strategy for a long, stable career at a large business.

For Attentive, we found three common areas of risk for our buyers: lost email revenue, legal regulatory concerns, and consumer annoyance. For each of these issues, we built a product to overcome the problem. For email revenue, we created sign-up units that collected both sms and email. For legal, we built a compliance product that actually turned into a great differentiating feature. For consumer annoyance, we built in automated functionality to control the number of messages a consumer received. These products helped reduce risk but also added to our overall product differentiation.

Reducing Time

A second really important source of friction is time. How much time does it require for your buyer to use your product? Is it time they enjoy? Do they need to do something in order for you to continue to generate money from your buyer?

For Attentive, we break down our buyers' time into three buckets: decision time, integration time, and maintenance time. Decision time is spent in order to make the decision on using your product. Integration time is how long it takes to implement and try your product. Maintenance time is how long to continue using your product on an ongoing basis.

To reduce decision time, we lowered the commitment significantly for trying the product. We created a completely free trial with no obligations of any kind. The trial only started when the customer activated the product, so customers could sign up for trials without concern about a lengthy integration process.

Integration time can be a huge issue for many products, especially enterprise software. Some businesses take many months if not quarters to implement a new product. With Attentive, we built a lot of products to reduce the time and effort required for a customer to integrate. This often included a lot of one-off custom programming from our team to remove any work required from the customer to flip on our service.

Maintenance time happens later, but can play a part in the initial decision-making about your product as well as renewals of continued usage. For Attentive, it took a lot of time to use our product properly, and most customers did not know how to navigate the tools. As a result, we built out a service arm of our business to do it for customers. This service arm ensured customers used our products the right way for improved success, and also helped us to generate incremental revenue.

Think through all of the ways your buyer spends time in using your product, and you will likely find a list of ways, some easy and some hard, to reduce their time spent with your product. This will make it easier to pull the trigger and buy your product.

Eliminating Cost Barriers

In almost any buyer decision, cost is going to be a factor. For new product categories, it can be an especially tall barrier, because a business does not have a budget allocated to pay for your product or solution.

At Attentive, one of the biggest sources of risk was financial loss. Almost every customer did not have existing money to spend on software like ours because it was a new solution. To solve for this friction, we offered a free trial to all of our customers, including really big businesses. Once we experimented with a free trial, we saw a huge uptick in new sales and conversions. Try to find a way to offer a free sample of your product in some form or fashion.

CHAPTER 17
In-Meeting Sales Tactics for Success

You've scored a big meeting with a potential customer. You have made a thoughtful sales presentation, as described in the prior chapter, and you're ready to go pitch the client. Before making the pitch, remember, buyers will forget presentations, but they will remember salespeople. In the call, and through subsequent meetings, you should aim to create a trustworthy and lasting connection with your potential customer to increase the chances of them choosing your solution.

At Attentive, we use tools that record our sales and customer meetings (Gong) so we have a clear record of what we said and ensure we do the right follow-ups after the meeting. Inadvertently, in a few cases, customers have stayed on the call after our team has left the call and had their debrief conversations about our technology. Those conversations have been recorded, and we have heard the unvarnished feedback after the meeting.

In one particular case, I remember we had a call with a potential customer that had already selected another competitive vendor, but they were considering changing their decision to us. After the call, the customer talked about the meeting with their coworker and said, "That guy on the call who looked tired with the gray hair was the CEO. They were really paying close attention and listening to us. They seem to really care. We should go with them." Nothing was mentioned about the product, features, or statistics, they were buying the person.

Over the course of my career, I've created a list of tactics that I go to for sales meetings. In this chapter, we will review some of the tactics on how to prepare for each sales meeting. I even have a printout on my desk that reminds me of each one, as it's easy to forget especially when you're in the moment of a meeting.

Principles of In-Meeting Sales Tactics

1. **Turn on the video:** It's much easier to build a relationship when you show your face and humanize your position.
2. **Prepare, be early, and set up a good internet connection:** You may not need many of the materials you make, but you will have the right materials to win the business.
3. **People will feel how the presenter feels:** Be positive, happy, and comfortable.
4. **Always have a second person on a sales call:** A silent, no-video person who is there to listen and help around the edges.
5. **Write when they speak:** It shows you're paying attention and makes the speaker feel important and heard.
6. **Embrace the golden silence:** Let the buyer keep talking to uncover critical information that is sometimes held back in the initial discussion.

7. **Repeat back:** Confirm the buyer's points and questions by summarizing their perspective, often leading to clarifying statements.

Turn on the Video

You are sitting at home working comfortably in your shorts and a T-shirt. It's easy to consider just keeping the video off. But according to an August 2021 survey by Zoom,[6] activating your video stream has a big impact on engagement. Among all professionals, 67 percent say that turning on video increases engagement in a meeting. A verbatim quote from the survey summarizes this well: "Having video on establishes a more personal connection on the call." Furthermore, 70 percent of respondents said, "I feel greater trust between me and my clients/potential clients" when the video is turned on.

If you decide to turn on your webcam, remember to dress for your audience. If you are meeting with a more corporate professional company, wear more formal attire. If an informal company, dress casually. Either way, you should have a good background, be professional, and look into the camera. It's fine if they don't turn their camera on; you are the one selling.

Prepare, Be Early, and Set Up a Strong Internet Connection

You should thoroughly research before going into the sales call. If the meeting is set up by an inside salesperson, I recommend

6 "When Turning Video On Benefits You, Your Teams, and Your Business." explore.zoom.us/en/video-engagement-survey/.

having the inside salesperson take the first steps of preparation. Create a standard prep doc for them to complete ahead of the call. This is also good training for them if they aspire to do outside sales, like most inside salespeople do.

Once you get an initial prep doc from them, you should read it and do additional research to ensure you know who you are talking to ahead of the call. Is this person going to be knowledgeable about your solution area? Are they likely the right person? Are they using anything similar?

This seems obvious, but it's so easy to mess this up: Show up ten minutes before the video call starts. Have an internal invite that the inside salesperson puts on your calendar ten minutes before the call. I also recommend blocking off fifteen minutes after the call. This allows you time to be available if the call runs long. If the call ends on time, use the booked calendar time to send your follow-up note. It's always impressive when you get the follow-up from the salesperson right after the call occurred.

There is no excuse for having a bad internet connection. You need to make whatever investment is needed to have a crystal-clear communication line. It's extremely frustrating when there is a bad signal and you can't talk with the other person. Have backup systems just in case, like tethering your phone or a portable Wi-Fi device.

People Will Feel How the Presenter Feels: Be Positive, Happy, and Comfortable

Similar to public speaking in general, the audience will often feel how the presenter feels. If the presenter is nervous, the audience will get uncomfortable and feel bad. If the presenter is positive and happy, then the audience will feel great. Mood is a huge component of the success of your call. After a call, people will often just say "how did that feel?" or "that felt good." So, no matter if you are nervous or feel bad, just take a step back, take a breath, and give off as much positive, passionate energy as you can—and the meeting will go well.

Always Have a Second Person on the Call

In the last section we detailed all of the stuff going on in a sales call—and it's *a lot* of stuff. It's very hard to do an effective sales call on your own, even if you know the product and material cold. You want to take great notes, but you also need to present your product, stay organized, engage, and many other things.

I strongly recommend for all sales calls that you have an additional person sitting in on the call taking notes. I like to have the inside sales reps handle this role because it gives them more experience on sales calls and helps them to understand the process. They can then also help with some of the steps detailed below in doing the call follow-up, like the call report.

While you have a second person on the call, though, this role should be silent and their camera should be turned off. They should not be an active participant in the conversation. This is very important, because you want the buyer to talk a lot, and also to build a relationship with the seller. This is much harder to do if a third attendee is talking and taking up mental space for both people.

Additionally, I recommend using call recording tools like Gong or Chorus to keep a record of all of your calls. We use Gong at Attentive to record almost all of our sales and client strategy calls. It's extremely effective when reviewing prior calls and helping plan future strategy.

Write When They Speak

This one is a little weird . . . but personally I like to have a pad of paper and a pen to take notes when the other person talks. I like to show them I am taking notes by visibly holding my pad of paper and writing down when they speak.

People *love* it when you write something down that they say. It shows them you are listening, so why not show them you are doing that? If you want to go a bit more high tech, open up a Google Doc with your call notes and simply show it on the screen share during the call. The person will be able to see the notes you are taking, and they may even tell you edits or additional information when they see your notes on the screen. This can be a bit more risky though, as the documentation may lead the buyer to be less forthcoming in sharing private information. Also, please see my tip above about having a second person on the call to take detailed notes.

Embrace the Golden Silence

About a year after founding Attentive, we scored a big meeting with the marketing leadership team of a large public company. We flew down to their office in Texas and showed up with a bunch of donuts. After exchanging typical introductory pleasantries, the chief marketing officer started explaining why they were interested in meeting with us. She started by telling us about how they were impressed with our pitch, so they were interested in hearing what we had to offer.

At the end of her talking, though, we held off on replying, and instead patiently continued writing notes on what she had said. As a result, several times she would pause, but then continue talking, giving more and more information about the problems she was encountering. She explained some of her biggest frustrations with their current vendor, and what she wanted in a new provider. After about twenty minutes, we knew her problems, and we were able to focus our presentation toward the issues that mattered to her. Within a few weeks, we had won the business.

When your buyer stops talking, hold back all of those impulses inside you to immediately start talking back and just wait. Giving someone room to talk and share their opinion is great. It will make them more likely to enjoy the call and feel like you are listening to them. Secondly, when there is silence, they will be compelled to fill that silence. I've found that the first thing someone says is only half of the picture. When you wait, they will fill in the rest of the picture and sometimes divulge additional information they may have been holding back for some reason.

Repeat Back

I was in a sales meeting once where a client was explaining their top priorities. They said that geographic expansion was not one of their top priorities. I asked them to clarify why it wasn't a top priority, and they quickly corrected themselves that actually global growth was a very big priority, and then went on to explain each company and how much they were spending to grow in each area.

When someone makes a long and detailed statement that may also include some questions, there is an impulse to immediately answer the question. You are excited because you feel like you know the perfect response. Hold back that feeling for a minute and make sure you are getting the question right. One of the most powerful concepts in sales—but also in all of conversation—is repeating back what the person just said. For this I have to thank my executive coach, Matt Mochary, who is a strong advocate for repeating back and uses it incredibly well.

After the person completes their question or statement, repeat it back to them in paraphrased form to make sure you are getting it right. Sometimes they will say yes, but often they will respond back and add additional components to their question. By hearing you say the question, they get the chance to think more about the question and add to it. They also realize how intently you are listening to them, and they appreciate that deeply. Everyone wants to be heard.

CHAPTER 18
How to Close Sales

You just finished an engaging and uplifting sales meeting. You discovered that your potential customer has a deep burning problem, and your solution can fix it. You have a few minutes left in the call. What do you do next to get the sale?

In this chapter, we will review some of the steps and tips to turn a sales meeting into a new customer. This begins with the end of the meeting by asking for the sale and addressing clear next steps. It is followed by an immediate email with the meeting materials, and an easy pathway to help the client say yes and get started. You can also get more feedback, resources, and excitement by writing a call report to document your meeting to the team. Finally, remember, whoever wants the sale the most tends to get it, so think of anything you can do to differentiate yourself to the buyer.

Principles of Closing Sales

1. **Don't forget to ask for the sale:** You seldom get what you don't directly ask for.
2. **Make it easy to say yes:** Remove any blockers to an easy path to moving forward.

3. **Send Call Reports out to the whole company for every sales meeting:** It helps educate everyone on your team.
4. **Whoever wants it the most will win:** Never stop trying.

Don't Forget to Ask for the Sale

You seldom get what you don't ask for. When you have a product ready and you are selling, you must end the call by asking for the sale. I like to ask "Are there any reasons you wouldn't try this out?" Sometimes someone is able to say yes on the call. If someone says yes on the call, they are extremely likely to keep their word and follow through, as people generally like to uphold their reputation. If they won't say yes, then you can learn the remaining objections to the sale and work to solve those objections.

Oftentimes, a response is that "I like your product and sale, but I need to talk more to my team first to make a decision." This opens an opportunity to learn more about the decision-making process. Ask the buyer who is their team and what their process will be to make a decision. If you find out that they need to do some internal meetings, ask if you can schedule a call one week from then to sync on their team's feedback. I like to actually get the next meeting on the calendar during the call, as it forces the person to make a decision. In a teleconference world, everyone has their calendar in front of them and can schedule a follow-up immediately. If they won't schedule a follow-up, it's because they aren't sure they will proceed with you. This is an important sign! Ask them why.

Over the course of doing many thousands of sales meetings, the second most common issue I have seen is running out of time. The meeting has good energy, everything is going great, and you hit the end of your meeting. The buyer has to leave, and you potentially miss the chance to close the sale. As a result, please keep close track of time and give yourself at least five minutes at the end of that conversation. It stinks to have a great meeting then have it cut off at the end because you are out of time before you can close the conversation.

As mentioned in the product market fit section, if you are still searching for product market fit and have not built your initial product, then end your call with a clear survey. Ask the person to rate their level of interest in moving forward on a 1–10 scale, 1 being absolutely not, and 10 being that they want to get started ASAP. It's amazing how often someone thinks a customer is extremely interested, then they ask this question and get an answer below an 8, which is a bad buying signal. Follow up this question by asking, "What could make this into an 8 or 9?" You will often find the answer is the objection holding back the sale and you don't even have the product yet. Now you will have a better idea of what to build. I also like questions like: What did you like the most? What did you like the least? What is the biggest problem with buying this product? How much do you think it should cost?

Make It Easy to Say Yes

When you finish a sales call, you want to have a follow-up email that is sent to the buyer within twenty-four hours of your call. Optimally, your follow-up email is sent within one hour of the end of the call. This is extremely impressive to the buyer and can increase the likelihood of closing the sale.

In order to meet these requirements, you should have a template follow-up email written that can be slightly edited and sent to the buyer following the phone call. You can have a few placeholders in the template to personalize the content based on the notes you took during the call.

For example, your template could include:

- A bold claim for what your solution can do for their business
- A review of the problems they are dealing with now at the company
- A transition to how you can solve those problems with your product
- A clear ask for a next step as provided in the call
- Any relevant links or attachments
- Examples of other successful customers (if you have them)

Everything in the follow-up note should be self-sufficient. In other words, if the email is forwarded to an executive decision-maker at the company, they should be able to fully understand your pitch without having been present on the phone call. The note should be like an executive summary that can easily be used to get approval for your product.

Finally, make the actual process of becoming a customer extremely easy. At Attentive, we created an online sign-up form that could be filled out in less than a minute. I was surprised to see how many large businesses would simply fill out the form to get started on the free trial and avoid a lengthy legal process. If the customer did request a contract, we would send it over for digital signature, so again it was easy to say yes and get started.

Send Call Reports Out to the Whole Company for Every Sales Meeting

For several years of the company, at the end of every sales call, a call report should be sent to the entire company providing a summary of the sales call. These emails, often called "Call Reports," are critical to everyone at the company for understanding what the buyer is saying and how our product is being received in the market. These emails can be extremely motivating across the team, and they also help the whole team to feel transparency about the business.

> Example of a call report content might be the following:
> To: all@companyname
> Subject: CR: BuyerCompany—Size—Stage
> Email Content:

- **Company information:** basic info on the company like website, size, etc.
- **Deal stage:** see closing customer section
- **Tldr:** a quick summary of what was said in the call and next steps. Maximum three or four sentences.
- **Objections:** any major problems the client had
- **Favorite Aspects:** what they liked the most about the pitch
- **Attendees:** who was on the call

- **Transcript:** a detailed transcript of the call, as well as a link to the recording if needed

If you get in the habit of sending these for every call, it will have an incredible impact across the company, as everyone can learn from the buyers together if everyone agrees to spend a couple of minutes each day reading the emails.

After a few years, you may find that the emails can be focused to only go to a more limited set of people than the entire company. At Attentive, we sent it to the whole company for four years, and now it goes to a more consolidated, though still large, list.

Whoever Wants It the Most Will Win

What else can we do to win this customer? What other steps can we take?

A sale is never lost until you have given up on it. Usually the company who wins the deal is the company that wanted to win it the most, and therefore put in the most effort. Winning is a combination of following a lot of steps consistently as laid out in these chapters, but also going another step where needed in order to win.

Over the years, our teams have had countless war stories about crazy things we did in order to win a partnership. Simple stuff like flying out to a customer across the country on a moment's notice, and then flying back again. Staying up all night to complete a last-minute presentation, and delivering it in a leather binding. Bringing a particular customized cake to a meeting. Ultimately, winning is simply never stopping in the pursuit of the sale, and always looking for another way to succeed.

CHAPTER 19
How to Measure and Reward Sales Performance

You and your sales team are setting meetings, signing customers, and scaling your business. As your business starts to grow, you need to manage the activity that is happening across your team. How are you doing, and how will it impact the future of your company's finances and growth? You need to have an idea of your performance so you know how to adjust your team, expenses, and supplies.

In this chapter, we will review the common tools for measuring the performance of your sales team, and how to set the corresponding incentive structure. This begins with setting a process for tracking your sales funnel, and then continues with goal setting and regular reports. When implemented correctly, you will be able to take the pulse of your company in minutes and have a good estimate of the future for months if not quarters or even years out, which in turn will allow you to manage to optimal growth and success.

Principles of Sales Measurement

1. **How to create a trackable sales funnel:** Measurement is essential to forecasting your success and allocating your resources.
2. **Develop a drumbeat of reports and status checks:** You don't improve what you don't track.

How to Create a Trackable Sales Funnel

Years ago, I worked for a startup on their sales team. The head of sales hired a very experienced sales representative to go after some of the largest potential customers. Based on his experience, the salesperson got a very large base salary, a guaranteed bonus commission for the first six months while he was building his business, and a large amount of equity in the business.

Our head of sales ran a weekly team-wide internal sales meeting, in which each salesperson went through their active deals. Most salespeople would have three to five deals to talk about. In the first meeting, this new salesperson came in with over a dozen hot deals. I remember thinking, *wow, he is really good.*

In the coming months, though, the updates became a bit repetitive. The salesperson had the same list of customers. All of them were "almost done" but had some sort of holdup here and there. It was always delayed a few months for some reason or another, but still very much alive. After a year, this salesperson had not closed a single customer, and our head of sales had to do something. He fired the salesperson, and we were given his opportunities to see if anything was actually real. As you may have guessed, none of these opportunities had any real chance of signing.

In my experience, the expectation of which deals will close is almost always too high. Salespeople tend to be optimists, and they are also often rewarded for being overly optimistic. As such, I would recommend discounting any forecast by over 50 percent to account for that overestimation, and really push salespeople for the reasons they think a certain way about a deal. As mentioned earlier, at Attentive we recorded all sales calls, and we kept a history of all emails, so we could get the same information as the salesperson in most instances.

Every time you talk to a new potential customer, it is called a new opportunity. In the early days, you can just track these in a Google spreadsheet, but it can get complicated very quickly, and you will want to migrate to a CRM like Salesforce (the most popular) or Zoho (the cheaper one) relatively quickly.

Initially, the most important thing to track is the company name and the opportunity stage. Opportunity stage is a number given to the account based on where they are in the sales cycle. Here is an example of what some early sales stages might look like:

- **10 percent (demo scheduled):** A meeting has been scheduled to occur in the future with this company.
- **25 percent (good demo):** We had a positive meeting with the customer but there is no time line for a second follow-up call, requires work.
- **50 percent (great demo):** We had a great initial meeting, and a follow-up is scheduled, or the account is expected to provide feedback soon.
- **75 percent (verbal commitment):** The customer verbally committed to moving forward with us.

- **90 percent (signed):** The customer signed paperwork with us.
- **100 percent (live):** The customer is live with our product.

Additional information can be overlaid onto this data, especially if you use software like Salesforce or Zoho. For instance, you can track:

- Age of the opportunity: how long it has been since your first conversations
- Size of the opp: how much revenue you could expect if they signed
- Last update: when was the last time the opportunity changed, and what changed
- Commentary: what is needed in order to win

All of these things together can help you to put together a forecast for where you think your business will be in the coming months. In other words, you can estimate how many customers you will add in each month over the next few months. You can then plan your financial resources accordingly, and also update those forecasts to your team.

Most salespeople will offer some resistance to using these tools, as it takes time, and it also increases your supervision over them. I've found the best salespeople actually like to be tracked, because they are confident and want credit for all of their work. At Attentive, we compensated and judged performance based on the tracked numbers to ensure everyone kept their CRM (Salesforce) and other tracking systems up to date.

Developing a Drumbeat of Reports and Status Checks

Now that you have all of the process and data together, you need to set up an ongoing structure to check and adjust your performance. As your company matures, you will likely adapt your process to the needs and size of your team, but here are some good formational basics.

Weekly Sales and Revenue Pacing Email

Using the sales funnel tracking data described in the last section, we set up a real-time report of our team's sales progress against our internal sales goals. This report was also used to create a weekly summary email that was sent to the entire company. The summary email showed how our products were selling, and also provided some high-level feedback on what was going well, and where we were running into problems. These regular emails allow the entire team to listen to the customer feedback and understand the reasons we are prioritizing different projects or strategies.

Weekly sales meeting

Most small to medium businesses hold a weekly meeting of their entire sales team. The meeting includes the sales team, the sales leader, and also optimally the CEO and cofounders. The sales meeting offers an opportunity for a quick temperature check on how the business is going. Meetings start by looking at summary metrics on team performance similar to the report described above, but with more granular data on a per-person basis. For example, for each sales team member, we would see total emails sent to prospects, total customer meetings booked, number of accounts at different sales stages, and new customers signed. This created a bit of a leaderboard so that everyone could transparently see their own performance and how it compared to that of their peers.

After this quick metrics review, the meeting goes around the circle to get an update from each salesperson on each active opportunity. During this part of the meeting, it was especially helpful to hear firsthand from salespeople on what was working and what objections were common. At Attentive, our early sales meetings showed us how hard it was for businesses to get consumer SMS sign-ups, so we built a lot of tools to fix it.

CHAPTER 20
How to Manage Early Customers

You have identified a real buyer problem, built a winning solution, and signed your first set of customers. Delivering success as a small company can be very hard. Your resources are extremely limited, your products are the minimum viable to launch, and may be brittle and constantly breaking. How do you ensure the happiness of your customers and success of your business?

As a new company, your customer service is one of the most important aspects of your product. Your business is making first impressions with its customers that will often determine their lifetime view of your brand. Many businesses view customers as a cost center that is minimized as much as possible. While that might be okay for monopolies, your service must be excellent as a startup.

At Attentive, we chose to name our customer service team "Client Strategy" to accentuate our hope to be an extension of our customer's team. We overstaffed our client strategy team in order to offer an incredible experience to our customers. Furthermore, we also understood that additional service could fill in the gaps left by an early product.

In this chapter, we will cover how to manage your early customers from trial partners to brand fanatics. We will start by sharing some tactical advice on how to manage customers, and then consider some broader strategic angles like a service model for long-term success. And remember, when the inevitable big customer problem happens, use the opportunity to build trust with your clients through honesty.

Principles of Customer Support

1. **Solve for growth with unscalable solutions:** You can make short to medium decisions to facilitate expansion, as long you fix them later.
2. **Overinvest in supporting your early customers, treat your first 50 customers like royalty:** They will sing your praises and help your business scale.
3. **Use problems as an opportunity to build trust:** Embrace your mistakes and be candid with customers when you have issues; apologize and ask for forgiveness.

Solve for Growth with Unscalable Solutions

Until you reach large scale, you should embrace doing unscalable things in order to make your customers successful and allow your business to grow fast.

At TapCommerce, once we hit product market fit, our business grew quickly, adding over five customers in a short time period. We didn't have all of the technology built to automatically manage the complicated advertising of our customers. As a result, we had instances where something would change in the market and we could lose hundreds of thousands of dollars, sometimes millions, because of issues with our tech.

To solve for this issue, we hired an operations team that manually ran the advertising programs for our customers behind the scenes. This process was incredibly manual and tedious, but it allowed us to smooth over many of our rough edges while we built technology to solve for these problems. It was much easier to find additional operations team members to support clients quickly than it was to build, test, and deploy reliable software to solve the issues. Over time, we automated many elements of our solution, but our operations team helped provide a framework for testing and advice in building those automations.

Overinvest in Supporting Your Early Customers: Treat Your First Fifty Customers Like Royalty

Ensuring the adulation of your early customers is the most important part of beginning your go-to market growth. Why? Most buyers are risk averse. They do not want to buy an untested/unproven product with no customers. As a result, they will rely on reputation, like references and case studies, in selecting your product. You must develop reference customers as fast as possible.

The first step in developing reference customers is to identify them. There are a limited number of buyers who are willing to jump in and be the first to try something. Every opportunity counts tremendously at this stage.

At Attentive, we took big steps, sometimes crazy steps, to treat our customers like royalty. Here are some examples:

- **Analysis:** Rather than just providing reporting on our numbers, we would do significant analysis and package it into an easily digestible presentation that could be shared with the executive team at the customer.
- **Celebration of wins:** We congratulated our customers when they hit key milestones. This could be goals with Attentive, or even other public updates that they published in their blogs like an acquisition or new product. By celebrating these accomplishments, we remind the buyer of all the great stuff that is happening, beyond the ways to improve.
- **Supporting their business:** Attentive would always use our customers' products when putting together our marketing and client strategy events. For instance, we might give away customer products at our conference booths or provide customer products as part of holiday gifts to our partners. These little steps showed the large commitment we had to our customers and their success.
- **Customer summits:** We threw large customer summits on a regular recurring basis, sometimes in person and sometimes virtually, that celebrated the achievements of our customers, along with our own updates and changes. These summits are incredible for building trust with our customers, but more importantly, they build a customer community.

When a customer sees the way you will manage their business and relationship, they will be much more comfortable attaching their reputation to your business, and offering themselves as a case study and reference.

Use Problems as an Opportunity to Build Trust

Your early products are likely going to have tremendous amounts of problems. If not, then you may not be testing and trying things fast enough. As a result, you will have instances where things break catastrophically, and you need to figure out what to tell your customers. Use these challenges as an opportunity to build trust with your clients. Always tell the truth, own the problem, and offer generous solutions to make up for your failures.

In the first few years of Attentive, we had lots of bugs and issues. Early employees will remember one incident in which our whole platform was down for almost twelve hours during an important season for our customers. Will customers notice? What will they say? How do we handle it?

When we recognized the issue, we decided to email all impacted customers and inform them of the problem, along with our plans for resolution. As the problem wasn't resolved for many subsequent hours, we continued updating customers. Furthermore, I personally called hundreds of customers, along with our head of customer success, to apologize to the customer, and let them know we were working to fix the problem, and also to expect a generous payment for the issue. Some customers responded well on the phone, other customers yelled at us and told us to fix the issue ASAP, but all customers knew what was going on, and understood the way we were managing the issue.

After the issue was resolved, we calculated the potential impact to our customers and decided to offer an extremely generous credit, even if we never heard a complaint from the customer, but knew that they were impacted. The result was tremendous. Customers greatly appreciated the openness with which we disclosed the issue, our ability to take complete ownership for the problem, and our generous compensation.

We have continued to replicate this process with subsequent bugs, and the response is overwhelmingly positive. When something breaks, tell the truth and use it as an opportunity to build trust.

Part 6
Fundraising

Your most important job as CEO is making sure the company has money to continue operating. You can never run out of cash, or else your business is bankrupt. You must always watch your cash balance and give yourself ample cushion to pay your bills.

Most small businesses are able to start and grow without raising venture capital financing. Initial capital to fund operations comes from the founders, their family and friends, or loans from banks or even credit cards. This is called bootstrapping, and can be a great path for businesses that are not capital intensive, or which can generate profit early in their development.

Many tech companies, though, require significant financial investment in order to build their initial product, scale that product, and begin seeing revenue far before profitability. Furthermore, if there is a big potential market with lots of upside for growth, a company may choose to make aggressive investments in order to grow as fast as possible.

When it comes to raising money, many entrepreneurs spend the vast majority of their time working on the pitch deck. While the pitch is certainly important, it's 10 percent of the overall process. You need to find the right investors, understand their motivations, and remove friction at every step to provide the best financing options for your business.

I've found the most success approaching the fundraising process like a sales process. As such, this section details the process from explaining the basics of venture capital to understanding your buyer's problem, then helps you to make a list of investors, build relationships, tweak your pitch, and run a tight process to raise a boatload of cash to grow.

CHAPTER 21

How Venture Capital Financing Works

You have found a great buyer problem, an exciting solution, and you need money to make your vision a reality. Before jumping straight into the steps to raise money, it's important to understand the broader venture capital landscape.

Over the past fifty years, venture capital has grown to an enormous industry, with many thousands of firms in the United States alone, and investments exceeding $200B+ annually.[7] As a result, the industry has gotten specialized and complex.

In this chapter, we will cover a high-level overview of the entire venture capital landscape. We start with a glossary of many of the venture capital terms you will hear when doing a fundraising process. Then we will dig into a quick overview of the ecosystem, and finally a quick introduction on what to expect when you run a venture process. Raising capital is a long and hard process. Hopefully this guide will make it easier for you.

---

7 Dealroom.co. "Venture Capital in the USA." Dealroom.co/guides/venture-capital-in-the-usa#:~:text=21%20January%2C%202023-,VC%20investment,35%25%20drop%20relative%20to%202021.

Principles of the Venture Capital Industry

1. **Glossary of Venture Capital Terms:** the basic words and phrases you will likely encounter when trying to raise funding
2. **Treat an investor like any other buyer:** a brief overview of how the system works
3. **Fundraising can take 90+ days:** It almost always takes longer than expected.

Glossary of Venture Capital Terms

Angel investor	An individual that invests their own money into companies, usually when the company is very young
Associate at a venture firm	A junior member of the investment team that is tasked with doing research and deal generation. Often they do not have decision-making powers but can be a good advocate.
Bootstrap	A company that has grown without the use of outside venture investment
Cap table (capitalization table)	A spreadsheet of the company's shareholders, showing how much each entity or person owns
Check size	The typical dollar amount that an investor will deploy for an individual investment
Convertible note/SAFE	A type of fundraise, typically used by early-stage companies that can facilitate a faster and simpler process, and may also avoid tricky topics like valuation
Deck	A PowerPoint deck providing an overview of a business for investment

Due diligence	Information about a company used to test the strength of the business and identify any weaknesses or concerns
Family offices	An entity that invests in businesses controlled by one wealthy individual or family
Limited partners (LPs)	Investors that provide the money to venture capital firms
Partner at a venture firm	A senior member of the venture capital firm that often has significant decision-making power or influence
Partner meeting	A weekly meeting or regular meeting, typically held on Mondays, where venture firms meet entrepreneurs and make investment decisions
Principal at a venture firm	A mid-level member of the venture capital firm that has influence but is not a full partner
Series pre-Seed, seed, A, B, C . . .	Names for the different stages of venture capital investment. Stages typically start at pre-seed, then seed, and then will typically count alphabetically with each financing round
Stock purchase agreement	The legal document and process used for most medium- to late-stage venture capital financing, through which an investor purchases shares in a company from the company directly
Strategic corporate investors	Investment groups that are based at large corporations
Term sheet	A nonbinding offer that outlines the potential investment between an investor and a company
Venture capital firm	An entity that makes investments in businesses using capital amassed from a variety of limited partners

Treat an Investor Like Any Other Buyer

Before jumping in to pitch meetings and closing strategies, it's important that the entrepreneur deeply understands the problems and personae of their buyer—in this case a potential investor in their business. There are many types of potential investors—venture capital funds, individual angel investors, family offices, strategic corporate investors, and more. Each of these groups has different motives and processes, so it's important you understand them. It can be a very complicated sale! The most prolific of these are venture capital firms, and probably the best place to focus your efforts.

Background on Venture Capital Funds

Venture capital funds invest money into new and growing companies. There are many mechanisms for investment. At the most basic level, investors buy stock in the company in order to own part of the company. Their goal is to see the value of the stock price per share increase, just like you would see a stock price increase on the New York Stock Exchange, so they can make money.

Venture funds can operate across the stages of a business—from the founding of the company up until the company goes public via an IPO. Funds will invest as little as $25K and as much as hundreds of millions of dollars in an investment. Different funds tend to focus at different stages of the business. The earliest funds are often called "pre-seed" or "seed" investors. They are investing at a point when the business is just getting started. As a result, the amount of money invested (often called the check size) is small—as is the value of the business. After pre-seed and seed investments, the remaining investments match the alphabet—Series A, Series B, Series C . . . and so forth. With each series, typically the amount of investment, and hopefully the valuation, increases.

Venture capital funds get their money primarily from Limited Partners, or LPs. These LPs can be rich individuals (sometimes called family offices when really rich), or they can be large institutions like pension funds, university endowments, and fund of funds (aggregators of funds). When a venture capital fund has been really successful, the funds will also often include a good deal of money from the partners in the venture funds.

Venture Capital funds typically raise a fund with a total dollar amount they wish to invest (say $200M) and a period with which they want to be able to return the capital back to their investors. Most funds raise capital into a fund, invest that money for a couple of years, and then hope to be able to return the capital (at a higher value) to their investors within ten years. Throughout the course of the investment, the funds will publish updates on the performance of their investments. They will also host intensive reviews of their investment portfolios with their limited partners, and spend extra time explaining performance and strategies to their largest investors.

Venture Capital firms make a lot of money for investing the money of their Limited Partners. They typically charge their limited partners an annual management fixed fee (for instance 2 percent), and a performance fee in which they get a cut of the profits (say 20 percent of the profits). In Wall Street shorthand, this would be referred to as "two and twenty," and is also a common fee schedule for investments in other vehicles like hedge funds. So if a venture fund raised a $200M fund, they would earn $4M per year in management fees investing the money. If the fund returned $400M to investors (with $200M in profit), they would make $40M in performance based fees. $80M total earned over the course of the fund, not a bad business!

As a result, the venture capital partners want to make sure their customers (limited partners) are happy, very happy. Furthermore, a lot of their money is probably coming from pretty conservative investors—like pension funds or university endowments—so they want to avoid anything that would embarrass the investment fund, and thereby their limited partners.

Venture funds live or die by the continued investment of their limited partners. If the limited partners do not like the actions of the fund, or the returns of the fund, they will simply stop investing. If new investments from LPs stop, then the venture capital fund will no longer be able to make new funds and investments and will simply cease to exist. This happens all the time—and the remaining investments will often be referred to as a "zombie fund," since the investor still owns positions but is no longer "alive," or in other words making new investments.

So the lesson here is that venture capital funds exist to keep their limited partners happy and make lots of money. The core problem is that venture capital firms need to invest in things that will produce a great return, but will also not upset or embarrass their limited partners. So how do they decide what investments to make?

Decision Process in a Venture Capital Firm

You may initially meet with associates or principals. They provide the first line or second line of review on a business before engaging a partner. On average, I would expect a business to have a minimum of two meetings with a partner before they are invited to the partner meeting.

Most investment decisions at a venture capital firm come from a committee of partners within the firm. For many firms, every Monday the partners in the firm meet in order to hear pitches from entrepreneurs and decide on which investments they choose to make. These pitches are often called "partner meetings" and are a requirement for most venture capital firms.

Getting to the partner meeting is the biggest step for an entrepreneur. An investment firm may look at a hundred potential businesses, but only invite one of them to present at their partner meeting. Of companies that present at the partner meeting, maybe 50 percent of those companies are presented with a term sheet to make an investment—so if you make it to the partner meeting your odds are pretty good. In order to get to the partner meeting, you will likely have many prior meetings along with requests for additional data about the company, called diligence.

In the partner meeting, the entrepreneur will provide a pitch of their overall business, and the details of the potential investment round. Depending on the maturity of the business, this process could be extremely formal or informal. The partnership may then ask a series of questions about the business, spending time on areas in which they are concerned or interested.

After the partner meeting, many firms conduct a formal vote to determine whether or not the firm wishes to invest. This voting process differs from firm to firm, but the bottom line is that someone will need to be really excited about your investment to push it to the finish line. In most cases, that champion will be someone whom you have already met with several times earlier in the process, which we will detail more below.

Angel Investors

When an individual makes investments independently using their own money, they are called an angel investor. Angel investors are most often involved in making investments in early-stage companies (like pre-seed, seed, and series A), but may also get involved in later stages. The investment size for angel investors can vary significantly—all the way down to $5k and up to millions of dollars.

The problems (motive) for angel investors are very different from venture capital funds. Angel investors often wish to see a profit, but they may also invest in order to gain insight into a given industry, support a friend or family member, or get some cool hats and gear from the company (on that note, I don't get enough hats and gear from the investments I have made).

Angel investors will generally make their decision very quickly. There are many factors they might consider, so it's important to understand what is important to a particular angel investor. A few examples would be:

- **Are other people investing?:** If other investors are putting in money, particularly venture capital firms, that means the chance of success is much greater since the company will have more capital and more support.
- **Who else is investing?:** Angel investors often don't have the time or resources to do intensive due diligence

on an investment. As a result, they rely on the work and time of the venture capital firm to provide assurance that the company is a good investment.

- **Who is the team?:** Angel investors, like most early-stage investors, will likely focus on the background and makeup of the founding and management team. You can change a business's product and market, but it's very painful to change the team significantly.

In recent years, some angel investors have also started rolling up "syndicates," which allow a lot of small investors to make a large-check investment together.

Family Offices

When an individual makes a lot of money, let's say hundreds of millions at a minimum, then they may employ a family office. This type of firm is like a mix between a venture capital firm and an angel investor. The family office is using capital predominantly from one source (the individual's money), but employs one or many full-time staff to assess investments. As a result, they will likely have more due diligence than an angel investor, but they will also invest larger amounts.

Corporate Investors (Strategics)

When an established, late-stage company has a lot of capital, they may choose to also make their own investments in other businesses. This type of investor is often referred to as a strategic or corporate investor. Large-scale companies will sometimes establish an investment arm or innovation wing, charged with investing in companies that are interesting to the corporate investor.

Strategic investors have many motives for investment, and they may be far less interested in return on capital. Investments may offer the company early access to innovative technology, awareness of market trends, and branding appeal to be viewed as a cutting edge and modern business. Many late-stage corporate funds may invest in early-stage businesses which they believe may be developing products in an area in which they plan to expand in the future. By investing, they get to closely monitor the progress of the company, learn from them, and potentially also have the option of buying the business at a later date.

Fundraising Typically Takes More than Ninety Days

Fundraising announcements pop up in the media from time to time, with entrepreneurs telling stories about how they "raised capital in twenty-four hours," or "over a cocktail hour at a bar." You will often see get-rich-quick stories because they get a lot of clicks, but the reality is that behind most fundraising rounds is a tremendous amount of work. The fundraising process will likely take more time and effort than you expect it will.

For my first company, TapCommerce, we did fifty-two investor meetings in order to find a few investors that said yes. The process took about four months, with numerous false starts. Don't be discouraged when you hear "no"; it is a long process and you need to do a lot of meetings.

Seasonal timing can also be an important element for raising venture capital. Often investors, lawyers, and the world are on vacation in August and December. As a result, you don't want to start a fundraising cycle during those months or in the few weeks preceding those months. You can lose a lot of momentum that can be hard to regain. You will hear some investors say that this seasonality no longer applies, but I think it still mostly does, and you should act accordingly.

CHAPTER 22
How to Make a Venture Capital Pitch

So now that you know how the venture capital process works, let's get your venture pitch together. Similar to a sales deck described in the sales section of this book, the best venture pitch deck is changing over time based on feedback from the buyer.

In this chapter, we will help you to put together the basics of both your elevator pitch and the actual pitch deck. With the pitch deck, we will start by covering the tactical aspects like font, wording, and design to create the best possible finished product. Later, we will jump into the strategic aspects, like narrative structure to engage and excite the buyer. By the end of this chapter, you should have the building blocks to make your own stellar venture pitch.

Principles of a Venture Pitch

1. **Practice a great elevator pitch that is easily retold by a venture partner:** You need to distill your pitch down to less than a minute.

2. **Hire a freelance designer to make a professional pitch deck:** You want to put your best foot forward for investors just like you would for potential customers.
3. **Your pitch deck should be easily consumed:** Most investors will quickly scan through your deck in an email over the matter of a minute or two.
4. **Use your pitch deck to tell your story:** Create an appendix to answer objections.
5. **Don't expect any confidentiality in the pitch process:** Whatever you share will likely make its way to competitors and adjacent companies.

Practice a Great Elevator Pitch That Is Easily Retold by a Venture Partner

As an entrepreneur, you need to tell a story that is easily replicated, packaged, and delivered to all relevant decision-makers. The person you tell your pitch will need to explain this pitch to the other partners in their firm to complete an investment. Therefore, your goal is to create a story that is really easy for a venture capital partner to tell their partners.

A great elevator pitch for an investor will share a lot of the same story as your sales pitch, as we discussed earlier in this book. The main themes should be:

- What is the problem?
- How does your solution solve this problem?
- How big can this business be?

I'll provide a quick review of my last two companies to provide an example of this process:

TapCommerce

Problem: Companies spend a lot of money to make and promote their mobile apps. After six months, though, only 5 percent of people are still using the average mobile app. Retention is a big problem.
Solution: TapCommerce lets companies buy ads targeted to consumers who previously downloaded their mobile app but aren't currently using it. By running TapCommerce ads, companies can bring people back to use their mobile app, and make lots of money.
Size: Companies like Criteo are worth billions of dollars because they offer retargeting solutions to web-based businesses. TapCommerce will be like Criteo, but for mobile applications.

Attentive

Problem: Companies are struggling to communicate with their customers. The average click-through rate on email marketing has decreased by 75 percent over the past eight years.
Solution: Attentive is personalized text message marketing, built to drive 10X higher revenue per message than email marketing.
Size: Over the next five years, SMS marketing will be the predominant way that businesses communicate with their customers. Email marketing saw the creation of many billion-dollar businesses like Mailchimp (acquired by Intuit for $12 billion) and ExactTarget (acquired by Salesforce for approximately $3.5 billion); SMS will be the same and potentially even bigger given the adoption of mobile commerce.

You can use the problem, solution, and size structure to create your own elevator pitch. Once you make the pitch, practice it over and over again, both with people and by yourself. You will recognize what works and doesn't work, and end up tweaking it to perfection. Schedule your first pitches with your least important investors. This gives you a chance to get the pitch great. I've found that my best pitches typically come at the end of the fundraising process, so I try to stack the best investors near the end.

Hire a Freelance Designer to Make a Professional Pitch Deck

Some of the best money you can invest in an early-stage company is to hire a freelance designer to help you to make a good-looking pitch deck for investors. When you don't have numbers, your pitch is all about a story (but you should also figure out why the numbers aren't good before you raise money). A professionally designed deck shows the audience that you are good at telling a story, and implies that your company is professionally run.

I recommend using tools like Upwork to hire a freelance design consultant. For less than a thousand dollars, you can have them design for you a consistent deck template including a color palette for your brand, a decent corporate logo, and custom graphics for any charts or diagrams you wish to include in your presentation. These seem like small things, and I'm sure you might say to yourself, *I can do it on my own just fine, my work looks fine*. I've said those lines—and let me tell you—it's much better if you get a designer to do it.

Your Pitch Deck Should Be Easily Consumed

Imagine the way a typical investor is going to review your pitch deck. They will be sent a link to review your deck via a text message or email. They click on the link and quickly scan through the deck. I've used tools to measure typical engagements from investors, and found that the average investor will view the deck on their mobile phone and will only spend one or two minutes *in total* reviewing your deck before they make a decision of interest.

This means you need your deck to be extremely scannable from a mobile device. Slides should have:

- A big headline of each slide, with each slide representing one idea
- Large fonts (minimum 16 points), and a maximum of three bullets per side of text
- At least half the slide is an image or chart, and half the slide is text. In some cases, the entire slide is a chart or image.

The only slides in which I might deviate from this is when talking about product features, as it helps imply the complexity of your product a bit, but even then I wouldn't overdue it.

Hopefully with each pitch it is getting a little better, and you actually want to meet with your best targets last in the process so you have a calibrated pitch.

Use Your Pitch Deck to Tell Your Story and Create an Appendix to Answer Objections

The pitch deck should mirror a lot of the same content as your sales deck, but include a few extra items that the investor is looking for. Here is a run-through of our fundraising deck for the Series A in Attentive, which includes both the script used in the meeting and an explanation of each slide. I hope this helps in creating your own pitch deck.

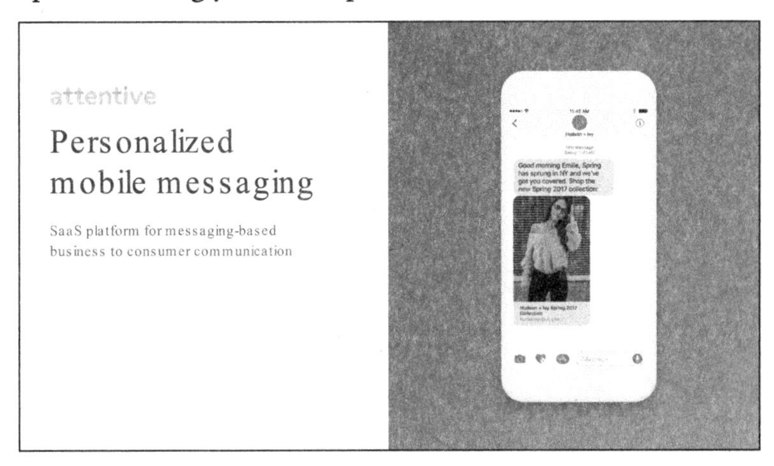

Cover Slide

Script:
Thanks again for taking the time to meet with us. Attentive helps businesses to make a lot more money with our text message marketing platform. We believe the future of customer marketing and communication will happen via text message, and today, we will show you why customers are choosing Attentive.

Explanation:
It's important to ensure the investor knows exactly what the company does at the start of the meeting. While some people

in the meeting may be familiar, you have to assume several are not prepped in any way. Remember to explain the business in terms of the problem it solves.

People/Introductions Slide

Script:

I'm Brian Long, the CEO and cofounder of Attentive, and I'm also joined by Andrew Jones, our VP of Product and cofounder. Andrew and I have started many businesses together, including our last business, TapCommerce, which we sold to Twitter in July 2014. We have assembled an all-star team of the best people we have worked with over the last decade in the SaaS technology businesses.

Explanation:

I like to start with a People slide because it is natural to introduce our team at the beginning of the pitch, and it's also often one of the most important components for an investor to consider the business. It also tells a bit about the founding story, which builds an engaging narrative for the meeting, and something the investor can tell their partners.

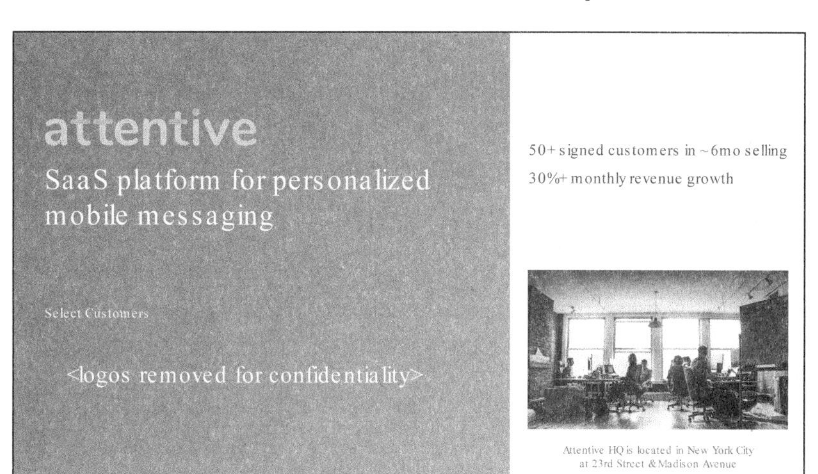

Elevator Pitch Slide/Traction Engagement

Script:
So again—our business is a mobile messaging platform. Companies use Attentive to market to and communicate with their customers. And we are growing really fast. In just about a year since starting, we have built an initial product, and scaled it to over fifty customers with 100 percent retention of paying customers and more than 30 percent monthly growth, reaching over $1M in annual revenue run rate this Q1.

Explanation:
This is your elevator pitch. You have a minute or two to convince the investors to pay close attention to the rest of your presentation. After just a few slides, they are already making decisions on their level of interest. You want to excite them.

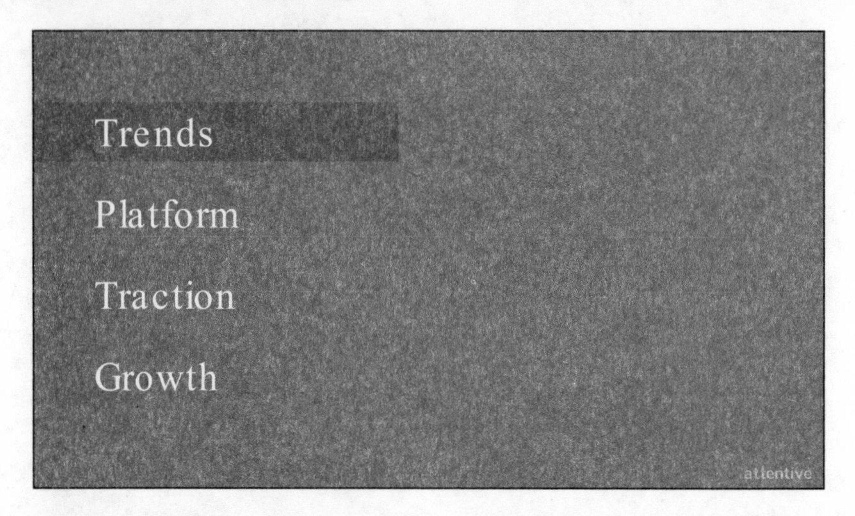

Agenda Slide Intro

Script:
In this presentation, we will cover some trends that explain the problem we are solving, and why SMS is growing so fast. We will then jump into our platform so you can understand our product today, then go into "Traction" to see how it is being received . . . and finally we will cover some of our plans for future growth. Does that sound good?

Explanation:
I really like having a clear agenda so that the viewer knows where they are in the story, and it's also easier for me to present and keep a clear structure. This basic structure uses similar tactics described in our earlier chapter on sales deck creation. The Trends section describes the customer problem. The Platform section describes your product's solution. The Traction section is the business results to date, and the growth section is where the business is going, and tells a bigger vision.

The agenda slide and structure also helps investors know what to expect so they can wait on certain questions for when we reach those areas. If an investor is interested, they will likely pepper you continuously throughout your presentation. This is normal and a good thing. You should be more concerned if they are silent, as this likely means they are not interested.

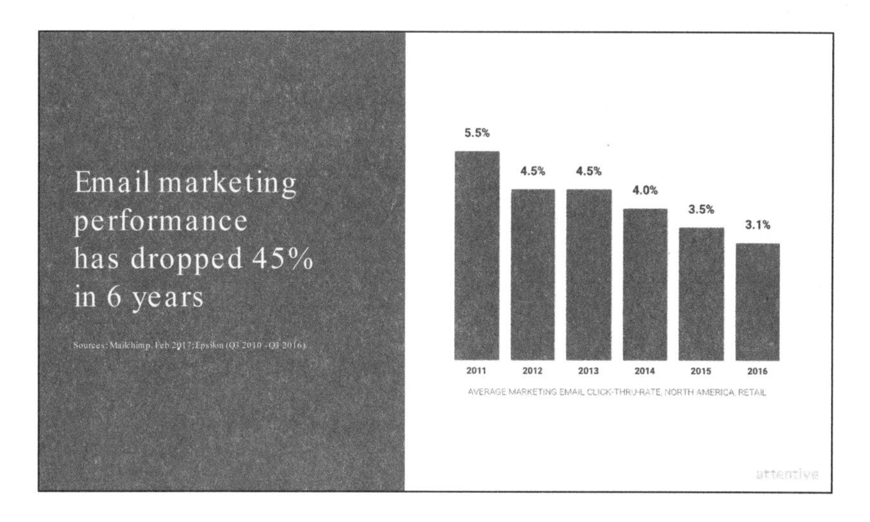

Trends—Problem Slide

Script:

Over the last six years, email marketing click-through performance has dropped by almost half. Performance is down, because marketers are sending more and more emails, creating lots of noise for consumers. This is a vicious cycle where marketers send more to fill the gap from bad engagement, and the result is even worse engagement for everyone over time. This chart will keep going down.

Explanation:

I typically use the first slide of the trends section to explain the core buyer problem. In this case, the problem is that the existing solution is degrading significantly in performance.

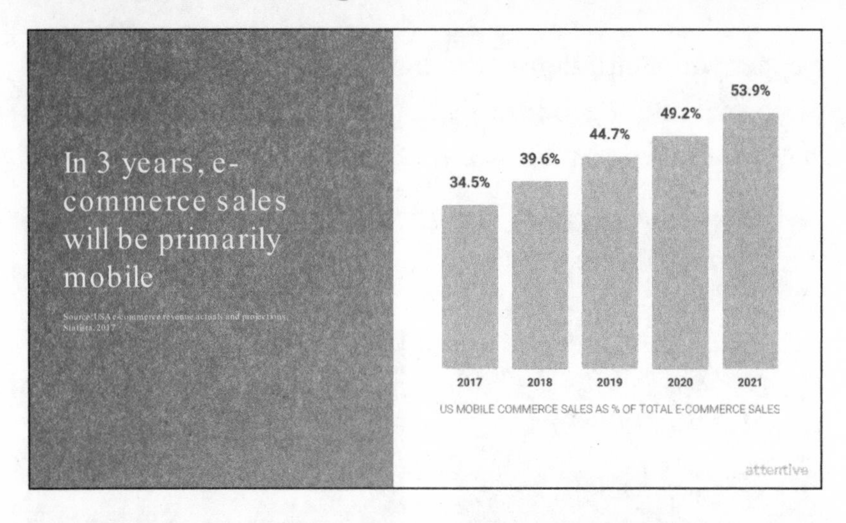

Trends—Transition Opportunity Slide

Script:

At the same time, the consumer is moving to mobile devices, where revenue is growing tremendously.

Explanation:

Before jumping straight into our solution (SMS marketing), I like to transition a bit by explaining a little more on what led us to SMS. In this case, the migration of customers from desktop to mobile devices has helped drive that change.

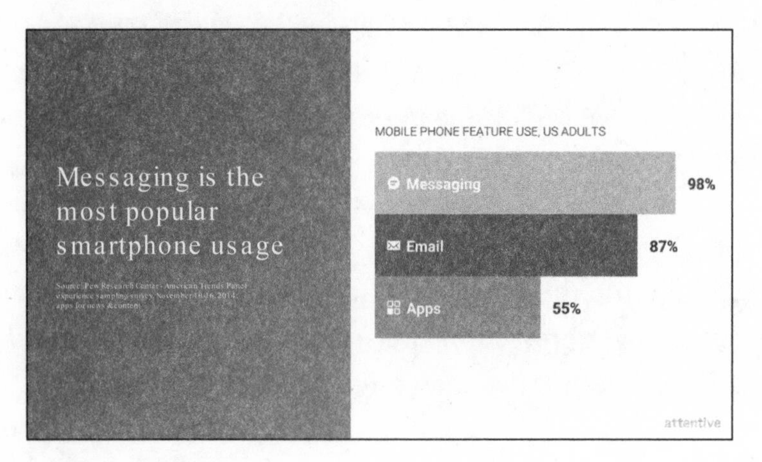

Trends—Solution Slide

Script:

And messaging is the most popular usage on mobile devices. Everyone knows how to do it, and it is ubiquitous and preinstalled in every smartphone.

Explanation:

Thanks to the prior transition slide, we can smoothly introduce our solution with a nice narrative.

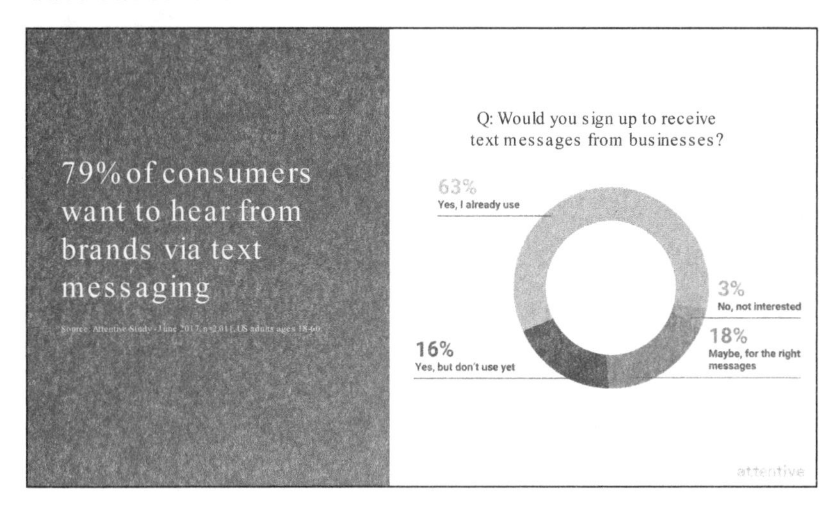

Trends—Solution Objection Slide

Script:

And the vast majority of consumers want to hear from businesses via text messages.

Explanation:

It can be helpful to understand the main objection investors will have to your pitch and deal with it early in the presentation. For Attentive, investors were concerned that consumers would not sign up to get text messages. This slide explained that the modern consumer actually wanted to get text messages. We couldn't find a third-party stat to prove this point, so we actually ran our own survey across ~2,000 consumers. We just posted a link on classified sites to take the survey.

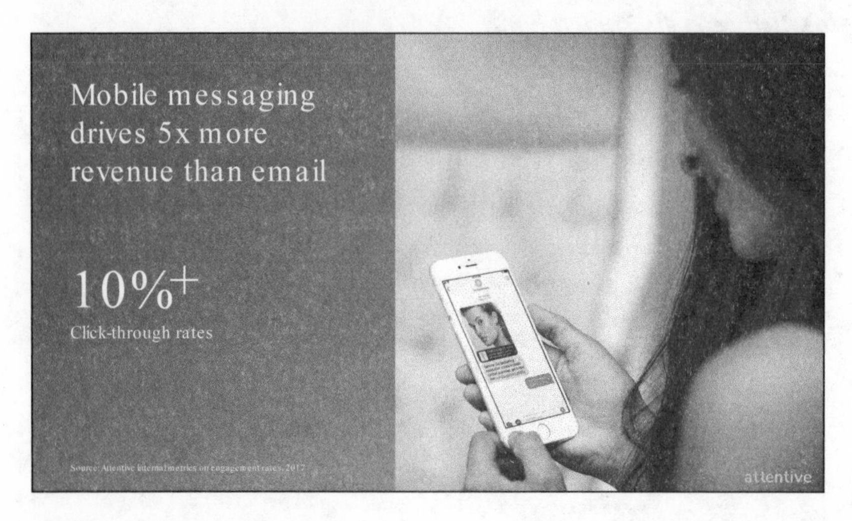

Trends—Solution Results Slide (Product Segue)

Script:
And the results speak for themselves. Today we estimate that almost every text message is read (you probably read almost all your messages), and we are seeing over 10 percent of people clicking on the links in the text messages we send. This is over 10X higher than the results seen in email marketing.

Explanation:
This slide is a transition between trends and our platform, so we have data about consumer solution usage, but it is moving more directly in the direction of the results from our platform, which allows us to cleanly segue to our platform.

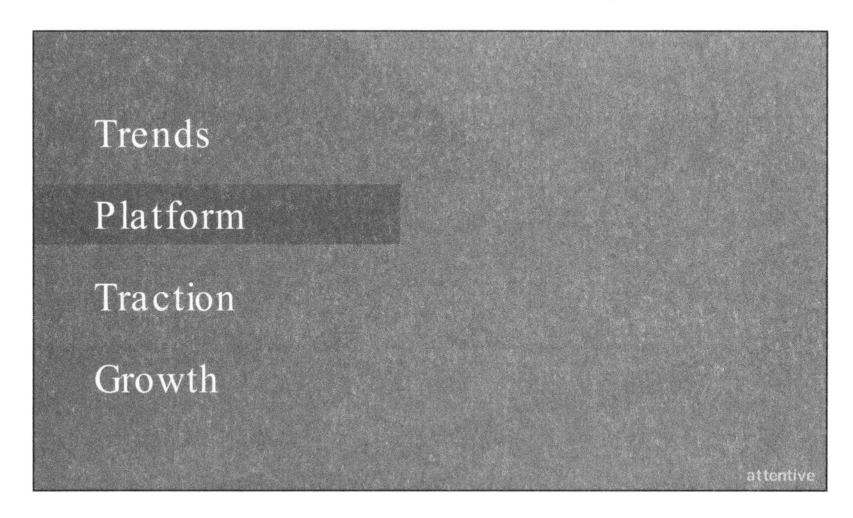

Agenda—Platform/Check-In Slide

Script:
Any questions on Trends before we jump into our platform?

Explanation:
I like to check in with the investor throughout the pitch to hear their feedback. This allows me to answer any concerns or objections they may have and also augment the future slides based on their feedback.

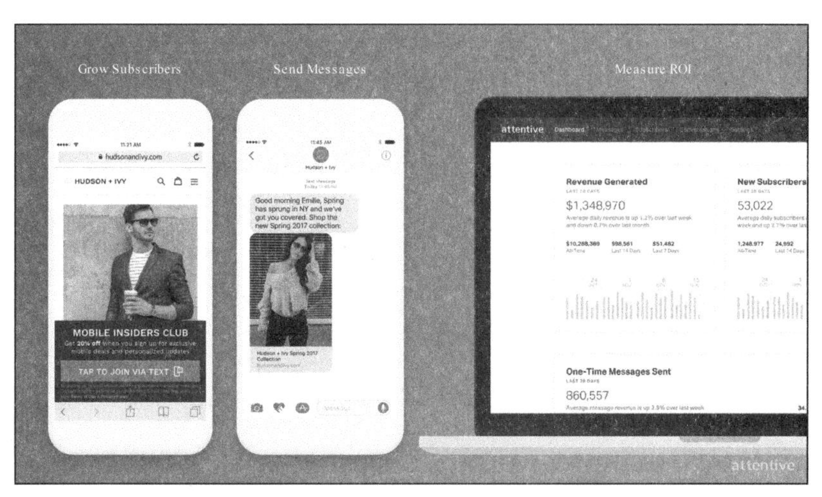

Product Overview

Script:
Our platform gives a customer everything they need to start and manage an SMS marketing program. We break it down into three areas: tools to grow SMS subscribers, send SMS messages, and measure ROI.

Explanation:
By the end of the presentation, you want the investor to be able to pitch your business to the rest of their partners. As a result, it's important that the solution and product are really easy to understand. I have tried to simplify these slides so they are easily consumed and explained with minimal text.

Note: I have excluded several additional platform slides from this book, but in the actual presentation we had five more slides explaining each component of the product. Investors love to dig into the product so they can explain to their other investors and feel like they really understand the business.

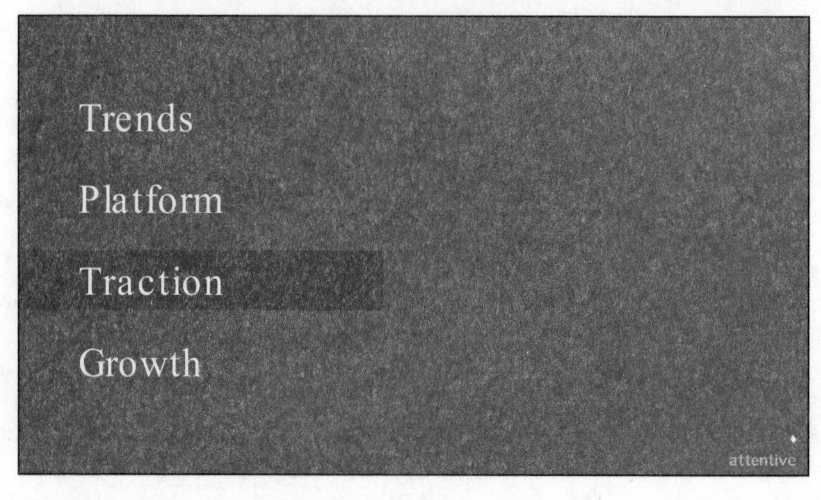

Agenda—Traction Check-In Slide

Script:
Any questions on our platform before jumping into our traction?

Explanation:
Just another check-in opportunity. This one is especially important. Do they buy the solution? Do they understand it?

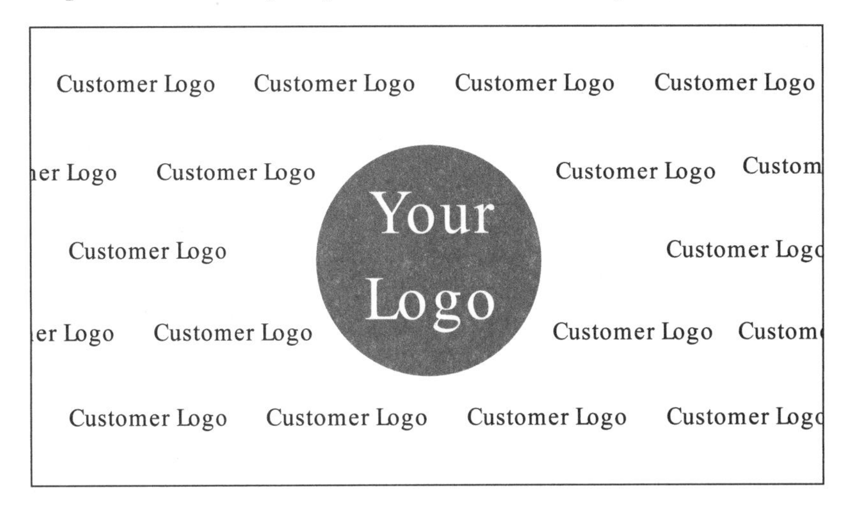

Traction Slide/Logo Slide

Script:
Our product has grown to over customers in a matter of months with exceptional results, retaining most customers.

Explanation:
Does your solution solve the buyer problem? If yes, then your buyers should be happy and see great results. Find the stats that show your solution is working and put them in the presentation.

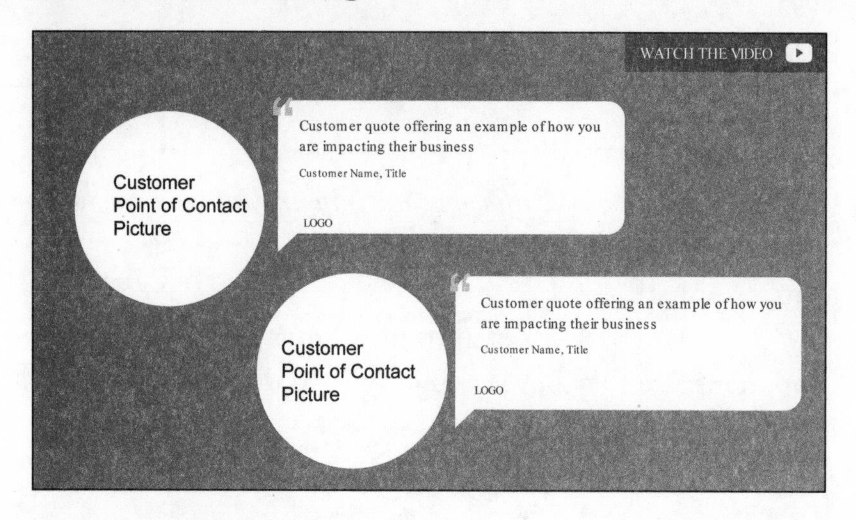

Case Studies Slide

(Actual customer faces and names removed for privacy)

Script:
And customers are quickly seeing this channel become one of their most important marketing and communication channels. In a few short months, it has become the #2 channel, and we see it being the #1 channel for many marketers in the near future as their lists grow.

Explanation:
Stats are great, but people also love stories. Try to include several case studies to explain how a particular customer used your product and the results they have seen. This storytelling can often be more engaging and memorable than just stats.

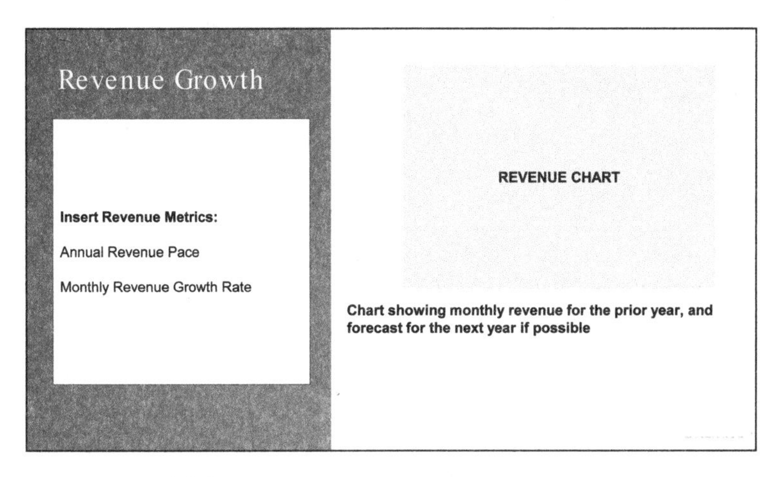

Revenue Slide

Script:
And you can see, our revenue has grown tremendously this year, and we forecast it to continue growing over the next several years, along with this detailed profit-loss statement.

Explanation:
I have removed the actual slide for confidentiality purposes, but investors will want to see revenue metrics when possible. Revenue helps the investor see a clearer pathway to medium-term scale and value from your business. It is also good to create a profit-loss statement for the next several years so the investor knows what to expect.

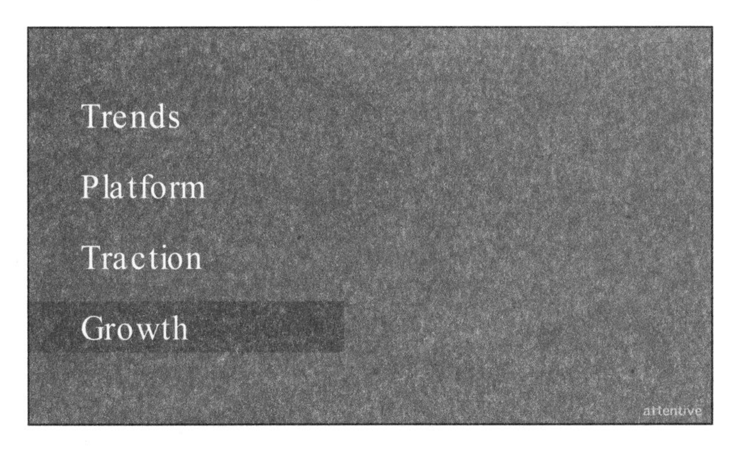

Agenda—Growth

Script:

And we are just getting started . . .

Explanation:

Although I "check in" on the prior agenda slides, I like to just flow right into Growth without checking in. Traction is usually pretty straightforward, we are late in the deck, and we want to wrap with a strong vision of where we are going.

Product Vision Detail

Script:

We are building the primary way businesses will communicate with their customers.

In five years, we will be managing all components of the customer relationship, from acquisition and sales all the way to reviews and customer service.

Explanation:
Tell your big vision for where your business is going. Investors want to understand the business today, but they also want to make sure you are going to an interesting place.

Closing Slide

Script:
So—I would really appreciate your candid feedback. How would you rate your interest level on a 1–10 scale? One being not a fit, ten being you want to give me a term sheet right now.

Why do you feel that way?

Explanation:
Similar to the system for rating sales pitches, I like to get a rating from an investor. Based on their answer, I can then ask follow-up questions to understand and address their concerns. This feedback is also really helpful in tweaking the pitch, and to ensure I focus my time with the most interested investors.

Don't Expect Any Confidentiality in the Pitch Process

You should assume that the contents of your pitch deck will be sent around extensively, especially to people that have similar companies. Why? Investors typically do not have expertise in the direct area of your business. They want to do research on the market before they make an investment. One fast way to do research is to send the deck and other materials to someone they know in the industry and get their feedback on the business. As a result, I've been sent a lot of decks and information about companies similar to the businesses I have founded.

Don't put your secret sauce or detailed future strategies in your pitch deck. Be careful about sending too much, especially if it's in a fashion in which it is easy to forward. My strong preference is to use a tool like DocSend that allows you to have some control over the deck. DocSend also has a password function to block the deck, along with tracking on who is viewing the deck, and the ability to remotely remove access after your process is complete.

I would also be clear with investors. If you don't want something sent to anyone, be very explicit. Tell them please do not send this deck to anyone outside of their direct general partners (note: no advisers). They may not keep their word, but many investors do care about their reputation. If you don't ask, you should assume it will be sent to a lot of people.

Remember that ultimately the deck is a teaser to talk to you. A venture capital investor is generally not going to make an investment without talking to the CEO, especially not a significant investment. Angel investors, on the other hand, may not require a call but they will want to see that other investors have done due diligence. But remember, if they never talk to you, they are probably a lot less likely to help you once they are on your cap table.

CHAPTER 23
How to Get Venture Capital Meetings

Now that you have your elevator pitch and a proper deck (by reading the prior chapter), it's time to start raising money. In this chapter, we will walk through how to create a list of potential investors for your business, set up meetings, and develop a champion to close an investment.

Principles of Booking Venture Capital Meetings

1. **Building your list of target funds:** Identify the investors that make similar investments to your business.
2. **Ask successful entrepreneurs for investor introductions:** I've seen great success by working with fellow entrepreneurs to get investor connections.
3. **Take the extra meeting:** The more time you put in, the more likely your fundraising will succeed with a great outcome.

Building Your List of Target Funds

The process of fundraising begins with building a spreadsheet of potential investors. According to PitchBook/VentureBeat,[8] over 1,000 venture funds raised a new fund in 2021, totaling over $150B in capital in just one year. Funds are typically deployed within three to five years of when they are raised, so the total universe of actively investing venture funds could be around 3,000 in the United States alone. Other websites like Crunchbase.com list over 25,000 investment funds globally. Funds, though, tend to be highly specialized and focus both on specific company stages and company verticals. For instance, a fund may only invest in later-stage (pretty big) healthcare companies.

Your first step is to create a spreadsheet of venture funds that have shown a history of investing in businesses similar to your business. Here is a process you can follow to build a list:

- **Get a big list of funds:** There are a number of providers of lists of funds like PitchBook, CB Insights, and Crunchbase. Personally, I have used Crunchbase.com to create a directory of potential funds. Just click on "advanced search" to start creating your list. You can then filter to match your business. For instance, if my company offers payment solutions, and we are raising our first round of capital, I can filter by "Type: Venture Capital," "Industry: Payments," and "Funding Stage:

8 Takahashi, Dean. January 5, 2023. "U.S. VC Investments and Exits Plummeted in 2022|NVCA." VentureBeat. Venturebeat.com/games/vc-investments-and-exits-plummeted-in-2022-nvca/#:~:text=VCs%20raised%20more%20money%20than,straight%20year%20exceeding%20%24150%20billion.

Seed" to get about 4,000 results. That's a great list, but it's still a ton of investors, so I should filter a bit more to find my best fits.

- **Consider filtering by location:** Location can be a very big driver of investment, as investors may be more likely to invest in a company they can readily visit. For instance, many US-based firms are tasked with just making investments in the United States. Reducing your search from the prior section to just the United States outputs a list of 1,500 funds.
- **Look for similar investments:** You can also filter by similar investments. Make a big list of companies similar to yours, which you may have encountered while doing your research in the "Product Market Fit" chapter. You can input these into "Invested in" to filter down. Note that you may want to just target similar companies and not direct competitors, as some venture firms will not make investments in directly competitive businesses. For instance, I added "PayPal," and reduced the list to just four funds. Please add a column to your spreadsheet with the names of the similar investments the fund has made when creating your list. This will be important in the next step of getting a contact.
- **Consider investment quantity:** Crunchbase also provides data like total investments made. This can be a really helpful dimension to sort against because logically investors with more investments will likely be easier to pitch on investing in your business.

Now that you have a big and filtered list, I like to track my status as I work through each one. For each firm, you want to develop a primary point of contact. So how do you identify and connect with someone at each firm?

Ask Successful Entrepreneurs for Investor Introductions

Early-stage investing is built on trust. An investor is giving a big stack of money to a single person or a small group of people, and trusting them to work hard to deliver a good return. As a result, I've found most investors are hard to reach by cold emails or social media messages. Instead, they prefer to work with people that are introduced from someone they already trust. Most of my investors have come by being introduced by a friend, colleague or fellow entrepreneur.

Entrepreneurs are my favorite way of starting the fundraising outreach process because they are incentivized to introduce you to investors. If you find one entrepreneur who has experience raising money in your industry, there is a good chance they know a lot of investors who are relevant to you. Entrepreneurs occasionally reach out to me to ask for an introduction to one of my prior investors. If the company seems like a good idea, or the entrepreneur has written a nice note, I'm happy to forward it to my investor. The investor may not be interested, but they are quite likely to read the email and consider it.

Now go back to the list you created of target investment funds in the last step. Consider starting your outreach by emailing startup entrepreneurs who have worked with the investor. For each firm, you should be able to find their list of recent investments on Crunchbase. Go through the list, and email/direct message all the founders of each investment. Include a short note along the lines of this:

Subject: Thoughts on [Investor Name]
Content:
Hi [Entrepreneur name],
Congrats on [Company Name]. My company, [Company], is currently fundraising and I noticed [Investor Name] invested in you. Have you had a good experience?

If yes, would you mind forwarding this note to them to see if they would be interested in my company? Here is a quick description:
[2–3 sentences describing your company]

Thank you!
[Your Name]

Separately, you might also just ask the entrepreneur for a brief call or to get a coffee. You may find more success by building a relationship with them first before asking for an introduction. If your goal is to get three introductions from each person you meet, very quickly you could have a ton of potential investors in your fundraising process.

If you can't find any similar investment entrepreneur to email for a particular firm, then you can always just send an email or social media direct message to the members of the investment firm directly. You will likely have more success sending cold messages to lower-level members, like associates or principals, rather than partners. Low-level employees are typically focused on finding new opportunities, whereas partners have to spend time on lots of other things, including managing their existing investments, communicating with their limited partner investors, and deciding on investments that are at the end of the process.

Take the Extra Meeting

Like any other sales process, raising venture capital is a numbers game. The more investors you engage, the more likely you are to find someone who is interested in learning more about your business. So it's time to put in the work. You can spend several weeks just running the process described in the last two sections. You can build a big list and work your way through piles of investors to find one success.

My series A fundraise for TapCommerce was long and filled with failures. It took about four months from beginning to end. We connected with dozens of firms. After many firms said no, we finally had a firm say yes and sent us a term sheet. I was ecstatic. The price was a bit low, but seemed fair. I was just about ready to sign, then I got an offer to travel to an investor in Boston the next day. This investor had looked at our seed round, but decided not to invest. It seemed like a waste of time, but I accepted the meeting and jumped on the next train to Boston.

Once in Boston, the meeting started small, but was quickly joined by several partners in the firm. After a couple hours of questions and conversation, the investor presented me with a term sheet at their office. The price was twice as high as the other term sheet! It was worth the extra trip. I've experienced this now many times, and the simple lesson is take every possible meeting until the end, as I've often found the unexpected deals come through, and the ones you may be expecting do not.

CHAPTER 24

How to Manage the Venture Capital Process Post-Pitch

Managing a venture capital process can be compared to herding cattle across a vast wilderness. You are constantly working to keep everyone together. Ideally, you want all of your investors to reach the end of the process at the same time. By doing this, you will be presented with several competing offers at the same time, and you can smoothly negotiate the offers against each other for the best possible outcome.

In this chapter, we will review some of the steps and tactics for a successful fundraising process. We will dig into common signals, popular financial structures, and investment negotiations. Finally, we will remind the entrepreneur of the importance of trust in the investment process.

Principles of the Venture Capital Post-Pitch

1. **Inaction means "No":** When you aren't getting feedback it means that the firm feels no reason to move forward with your company.

2. **Early investments, like pre-seed and seed, will often use a convertible note:** Leverage boilerplate templates to minimize legal costs and expedite the closing process.
3. **Negotiate term sheets, and beware of weird terms:** Some investors are known to stick to one-sided rules that are difficult to remove from later financings.
4. **Never lie or embellish anything during the deal process:** Trust is at the center of the investment process for most firms.
5. **Be ready to provide additional diligence:** A clean data room is a great signal to investors.
6. **Don't celebrate or announce until the money is in the bank:** Consider waiting until it has a strategic advantage for your business.

Inaction Means "No"

When pitching investors we had an ongoing joke. When the meeting ends, if the investor says "congratulations on building a great business," and then wraps up the meeting, it means they aren't interested in investing.

As mentioned earlier in the chapter on product market fit, almost no one will give you critical feedback, so you shouldn't expect it from investors. Most investors will not directly say "no," unless you really push them for an answer. They know that a "no" is very upsetting to the entrepreneur, and thus could have them miss out on future opportunities or develop a bad relationship that hurts their reputation.

After a venture pitch, most investors will just congratulate and compliment you, explain that they will huddle on it, and leave an unclear time line. This type of post-meeting interaction means they are likely not interested in investing in your business. You may not hear anything more from them, or they may send you a note at some future point to say they are interested, but just not ready to do anything "now," but please "keep them in the loop."

If you aren't sure where you stand at the end of a venture pitch, consider closing your pitch in a similar style as a normal sales pitch, as mentioned in the pitch deck chapter. Ask the investor their interest level in investing on a 1–10 scale. Once you get a score, ask follow-up questions on why they gave that score, and what it is missing from being a 10. Let the investor really speak, and make it clear that this feedback will help you in the future, and you are very appreciative. This feedback can be a great gift if you can implement it to change your next pitch to another investor.

Early Investments, Like Pre-Seed and Seed, Will Often Use a Convertible Note

Over the last decade, it has become the standard for companies raising very early-stage capital to skip the process of a stock purchase agreement (SPA), and instead issue a convertible note to potential investors. The convertible note allows investors to loan the company money. When the company raises additional capital, the loan is automatically converted into shares of the company, with a couple of structures that are favorable to the investor as described:

> **The cap:** the maximum value that will be given to the company when the dollar loan is converted into shares in a subsequent financing

The discount: the percentage discount from the valuation of the subsequent round for which the investor's dollars will convert
The interest rate: the annual interest accrued on the loan that will also convert to shares
Investment amount: the total dollar amount investment

In an ideal scenario for the entrepreneur

- The cap will not exist
- The discount will be as small as possible
- The interest rate will be zero
- The investment amount provides 18+ months of operations

Of course the investor will want the opposite of these terms, and you will probably end up somewhere in the middle. As we will mention in a few chapters on legal operations, when in doubt ask a lawyer for what they consider to be the market standard to help set your negotiations.

Negotiate Term Sheets, and Beware of Weird Terms

For Series A, B, and later-stage investments, it is typical that the investor first shares a nonbinding term sheet. The term sheet outlines the important elements of a potential investment, which will typically be completed through a subsequent stock purchase agreement. If you receive a term sheet, congratulations. You should send it to your lawyer and get on the phone to go through each item to closely understand what is covered in the sheet. As mentioned in the next chapter, you should be working with a lawyer who specializes in startup companies and is very familiar with term sheets used by investment firms.

There are many important elements to term sheets, with new elements and market conditions changing rapidly, so it's important to get your counsel's advice. That being said, here is a quick review based on some of my experience negotiating term sheets:

- Investment amount: This is the dollar investment in the company. It's important to understand how much the investor is putting in personally vs. how much they are allowing other third parties to invest. It is possible you may have people on your existing cap table who have a right to make future investments in your company, so you may need to carve out space for them. *Overall, though, it is generally a bit easier and cleaner if you have one investor that is putting in over 50 percent of the round total.*
- Valuation: This is the value that the investor is placing in the company. This is usually represented as a fully diluted figure and converted basis—so that all warrants, other securities, and options are treated as common outstanding stock. *Generally, the entrepreneur wants this to be as large as possible.*
- Closing: This is when the investment will be completed. This will typically document what due diligence will be required to complete the investment. The entrepreneur wants this to be as fast as possible. Push for a two- to four-week closing time period. Four is probably the standard.

- Board of Directors: The board ultimately picks the CEO and thereby controls the operations of the company, so the balance of the board of directors is very important. Entrepreneurs should try to maintain control for as long as possible. At different stages, investors will push for one or several board seats, and at some point this will mean that the investors have more people on the board than the founders, and thus the founder no longer controls the company.
- Liquidation preference: This guarantees that if the company is sold in the future, the investor will get some amount of their money back. Market standard at the time of writing is a 1x liquidation preference (the investor gets their money back first), but you can see investors push terms like a 2x or 3x guarantee. *Entrepreneurs would love to have no liquidation preference, but a 1x liquidation preference is the market standard. Sometimes entrepreneurs push for high valuation numbers but also offer high liquidation preferences in return.*
- Voting rights: This indicates who controls what at the company. This can be a mix of immaterial and material decisions, and can get thorny when you actually draw up the documents.
- Legal fees: Most investors ask for the company to pay for their legal fees out of the closing. I know, sort of annoying, right? But that's the standard.

All in all, this is a lot of important stuff, so you need to make sure you have a good firm that is very familiar with deals of this type. Do not try to save money on your lawyers.

Never Lie During the Deal Process

The phrase "fake it until you make it" is popular in the startup world. During the product and sales section of this book, I described tactics in which you would test-sell market products before you built them in order to get market feedback, which is a common tactic across companies from early to late stage. I want to underline something very important about the investment process: You should never lie or embellish anything about your business in order to raise money. Furthermore, if you find that you have ever exaggerated or stated something incorrectly during the process, you should make it a point to correct yourself and provide the accurate figures to the potential investor. As the saying goes, trust and reputation are built over a lifetime and can be ruined in minutes. Venture capital is a small world.

The investment process is hard, and one of the most common questions you will get from an investor is "where you are in the fundraising process." This question should be translated to "Do you currently have a term sheet from another investor? Is there anyone close to giving you a term sheet?" The assumption from most investors is that you do not have a term sheet yet or you would have mentioned it, but they want to know how much time they have.

Investors understand that once an entrepreneur gets a term sheet, there is now a ticking clock on the fundraising process. The entrepreneur typically has a week or two to negotiate and accept the term sheet or decline the term sheet. By asking whether one currently exists, the investor can understand how much time they have to give feedback and determine next steps on a potential investment.

Getting the first term sheet is the hardest part and biggest step in the fundraising process. It is tempting for entrepreneurs to claim they have a term sheet when in fact they do not. Do not fall for this temptation, as investors are very likely to discover you are lying. Early-stage investing is built on trust, and if you lose that, then there can be no investment. On the other hand, I like to be transparent about where the process sits and embrace your status with the investor. The investor who provides the first term sheet is also the one most likely to win the investment, and thus they could potentially be ahead of their competition if you appear to be a good investment. In other words, they can feel special to be early and ahead of their competition.

Be Ready to Provide Additional Diligence

Before you start the fundraising process, it is important that you have already assembled some basic diligence materials on your business that can be easily shared with a potential investor. This shows the investor that your company is a professionally run business they will enjoy working with over the coming years. It also implies that other investors have already asked you for diligence, which is a promising sign of interest—as investors will often behave like pack animals, herding together.

I would recommend creating a folder at Box.com or Dropbox and populating it with folders and materials. I would divide these materials into two buckets:

1. Materials you can share before a term sheet:
   - Fundraising deck
   - Cap table (showing the ownership interest of the company)

- Financial forecast (any forecast you have of profit/loss over the next three years)
- Sales deck (if you have a deck you use to sell your product)
- Customer testimonials (if you have any)

2. Materials you will need after signing a term sheet to conduct legal due diligence:
    - Certificate of incorporation (likely from Delaware)
    - Bylaws
    - Other founding corporate documents
    - Any prior financing rounds
    - Employment agreements for all employees

Don't Celebrate or Announce Until the Money Is in the Bank

It may be tempting to celebrate your successful fundraising when you have signed a term sheet, but do not celebrate until your cash is in the company's bank account. After both sides have signed a term sheet, there is a period of legal paperwork creation and due diligence. Most term sheets are not binding in any way, and either party can back out for whatever reason. As a result, I have seen investors back out because of changes in the economy, issues in their own fund, or trivial issues found during due diligence.

Per my earlier point around due diligence, if you have already assembled all important documentation, and can provide it to opposing counsel quickly, you should be able to close the financing in two to four weeks. The faster the better to eliminate any market risks.

Part 7
Operations, Legal, and Finance

Behind the scenes of your successful company are lots of operations and processes to make sure your business runs smoothly. In this section, we will cover the basics of legal, operations, and board management.

CHAPTER 25

Setting Up Your Legal Structure and Processes

This section starts like you will hear many sections begin whenever legal is concerned. This section is not legal advice, I am not a lawyer, and you should seek legal advice before you do anything. With that disclaimer, I will lay out a few things that I would do if I were starting a business today, and how to manage early-stage legal operations. When legal is done right, it operates silently in the background to protect and support the business. Occasionally an issue may arise, but because you have the appropriate legal, it goes away quickly.

In this chapter, we will cover some of the basics on how to set up your business legally, create a strong set of base legal agreements for external and internal partners, and maximize the financial rewards for you and your team.

Principles of the Legal Ops

1. **Don't skimp on lawyers or it will be a big problem later:** Save yourself tremendous later headaches and potentially company-ending damage.
2. **Create strong employment agreements:** Avoid needing updated agreements or drawn-out legal problems later in the company's life.
3. **Consider longer vesting periods:** Go beyond four-year vesting to reward early team members with more equity over a longer duration.
4. **Carve out shares for family into your company founding:** Enjoy favorable tax treatment and present upside in the party without the downside risk.

Don't Skimp on Lawyers, or It Will Be a Big Problem Later

It sounds simple, but incorporation can be very complicated, as well as many of the issues that come up in the early stages of your company. It is absolutely imperative that you hire an experienced, specialized law firm to incorporate your business and to advise you through the life of your business.

In one of my first companies, we did a lot of the incorporation and legal through online firms, then we hired a cheap law firm for our first round of seed financing. Everything seemed fine until we did due diligence for our next round of financing for our Series A. As the amount of invested capital increases, you typically will also find that the amount of legal due diligence also increases. We hired new lawyers to help with the process, and we quickly found that our legal documents were a mess. We had to redo a ton of documentation and take a big tax charge personally and for the business. The due diligence process dragged on for weeks, and as a result, our bank account got very close to empty. We needed the round to close or risked losing the business, and didn't negotiate many important items toward the end of the investment process.

For Attentive, we invested in great legal from the beginning, and it has been very smooth sailing. If you are starting a technology company, I would hire a startup technology law firm. I have used Cooley LLC, which is great, but there are many great firms across the United States. They usually will not charge a lot to get the incorporation going in the hopes of making their money as you grow.

Create Strong Employment Agreements

A top law firm will have boilerplate employment agreements that all employees should sign without edit, including all of the founders. Documenting these agreements at the start could save you significant headaches and delays later in the company's history.

I have seen this done the wrong way many times, and it can be extremely expensive, and in some cases, even cause major investment deals to fall through. It can also be very divisive among the team and lead to grudges that linger and cause major operational problems.

Consider Longer Vesting Periods

Divvying up the equity at a startup is hard and awkward. There is a fixed amount of pie, so how do you divide it? Do all the founders get the same size slice? Do the early employees all get a big slice? The CEO needs to work with the other founders to determine your equity philosophy. Some companies provide a lot of equity with low cash-based compensation, while other companies provide the inverse. You need to decide what type of company you want—which may also be dictated by the talent pool you will need to hire and engage.

No matter the overall equity philosophy you select, consider longer vesting periods for your early employees than the standard four years. In the world of tech startups, most startups offer a one-year cliff, and then three years thereafter of vesting—and they do this for the entire life of the startup. The reality is that startups often take a lot longer than one year to get off the ground, and many often don't even experience massive growth for several years from their founding, if ever. As a result, you may find employees with substantial equity who have left the company before it has even begun its core business.

Instead of a four-year vesting period, consider a five- to eight-year vesting period. At Attentive, early employees signed on to five- and six-year vesting periods in exchange for more equity. Those employees who stayed with the company successfully for that time period earned additional equity.

Secondly, consider starting with smaller equity amounts with the promise to review additional equity allocations on a regular predefined basis. For instance, you could review performance for team members every six months, and consider additional equity allocations based on team performance. When providing new equity, you can issue it again over a long time period so that the employee builds an equity stack over time.

Carve Out Shares for Family into Your Company Founding

This is one of the better decisions I've made in company formation, so I strongly suggest you consider it too. During founding, your founding team should consider gifting shares or allowing family to invest a small amount when your business is still at a very low valuation during the incorporation process. It is very important to do this early on, then your family members will have very favorable tax treatment in the future, and they will also have a predefined portion of your company, which is a great way to include them in the ride if things go well. It is also nice because your family will be able to enjoy the financial benefits of your business success without a significant investment, or a feeling of awkwardness when you provide a significant sum later in the future.

CHAPTER 26

How to Prepare for a Board Meeting

In my early years as a CEO, I thought of board meetings as an opportunity to put our team's best foot forward each month or quarter. We spent a good deal of time making a great deck. We spent most of the meeting doing a walk-through of our board deck, which covered our positive results from the quarter, along with some few open questions. It was a rosy update on current operations.

While the meeting presented a positive picture of the company, it didn't really help our operations, and our management team came to view the meetings as a waste of time, and then we dramatically shifted our approach to board meetings.

The optimal board meeting will help the CEO and the management team to make critical business decisions. The CEO should view the board directors as helpful colleagues to provide feedback and direction for the business. The below guide will provide the best template I have found for running board meetings that build trust and generate meaningful actions as outputs.

Principles of Board Meeting Prep

1. **The Board Deck:** a balance of highlights, metrics, and core issues to review
2. **Pre-meeting video:** a short recording summary of the company performance, and the issues you wish to focus on in the board meeting
3. **Board survey and setting the agenda:** Create an open, written record of feedback to help steer board meeting content.
4. **Running efficient monthly call updates:** Keep a tight sync with your board and major investors to make sure they are knowledgeable about the state of the business and never surprised.

The Board Deck

As with most meetings, the most important aspect of a board meeting is the preparation before the meeting itself. Ahead of each board meeting, I share three things: a copy of our draft board presentation, a short video (using Loom) explaining the presentation, and a survey for all board members to fill out before the meeting. I like to share all of this three or four days before the board meeting. This provides time for your board to read the deck, watch your video, and write thoughtful feedback in your board survey. You can then use your board survey to set the agenda for your board meeting. Let's start by going through each element you need to make this possible.

A great board deck provides two things: a robust snapshot of company performance and a set of decisions and topics important to the CEO in order to run the business. The board of directors is seldom deeply involved in the operations of the business and likely does not have a detailed understanding of the company's position. This deck provides the board the critical context they need to help provide advice to the CEO for making decisions.

Today, as a late-stage company, Attentive creates a long deck for each board meeting consisting of sixty to one hundred slides. While the length sounds long, most of the slides are metrics and financials that are merely reports pulled from different internal dashboards and quickly updated each quarter. And while the deck length has increased over time, the components of the deck are relatively the same. We had a lot of the same core content when we were a small company and presented a ten-slide deck. Here is a quick review of each section of the draft board deck:

- Executive highlights: This section is a quick summary of what has gone well, and what has gone poorly since the last board meeting.
- Financials: basic profit-loss, balance sheet, and cash-flow statements
- Metrics: vary by business, but use the ones important to track your product market fit like NPS, Churn, and CAC/LTV
- CEO top of mind: Now that your company snapshot (highlights, financials, and metrics) has updated the board on core operations, it's time to get down to the real business. What are the top problems and issues for the company? What decisions do you need to make? Where are you spending your time? Share the issues you are dealing with and give the opportunity to get

help and feedback from your board. Typically I make a few slides for this, one or two problems per slide, along with additional reports and data to explain the issues.
- Department-level highlights and issues: Similar to your role as CEO, each department leader gives their own top-of-mind achievements and challenges.

Video Recording

Once you have completed your draft board deck, I like to record a quick video summary to accompany the slides that I send to the deck. I use a tool called Loom, which records my board deck, as well as my face and voice. In my board summary, I provide a very quick update on company highlights, then I jump into the CEO top-of-mind. I lay out the problems I am dealing with in each, along with some of the potential solutions for each problem. I then ask the board to provide their feedback in the survey mentioned below. The entire video is usually five to ten minutes long but eliminates the need to use valuable board time. I have also found a video can significantly clarify a problem and solution better than a simple slide or two can do on its own.

Board Survey and Setting the Agenda

The final piece of board preparation materials is a short survey. After reviewing the draft board deck and watching my video recording, I ask all board members to complete a quick pre-meeting survey. My questions in the survey change based on the content of the meeting, but typically you will find questions like:

- What is your name?
- For [top-of-mind issue #1, 2, 3]: Do you agree it's a significant problem? What do you think about our solution? Do you have any other ideas?
- Pretend you are the CEO of Attentive. What would you do differently?
- Do you think we are missing any top-of-mind issues? If so, what are they and why?
- What are you most concerned about for the company?
- Any other topics you think we should discuss?
- For particular questions, I may also ask for a rated numerical response rather than an open-ended response.
- How many months of runway do you think we should target? [number of months]
- How much do you like the new company positioning? [1–10 rating]

Spend time to think of all the questions you would ask the board, and ensure everyone fills out the survey before the meeting. These pre-meeting surveys also serve as an important written record of each board member's opinion and allows independent thought rather than the groupthink that can sometimes invade the board setting.

Running Efficient Monthly Call Updates

Board meetings should not surprise the board members but rather serve as an open area for conversation around the biggest issues the business is encountering. The best way to ensure continuous alignment across the board is to schedule monthly check-in calls with your board of directors.

For these monthly calls, I like to follow a format similar to the 1-on-1 templates detailed in "Managing a Growing Team." This means including sections for: recent wins, biggest issues, top three, and feedback. For these one-on-one calls, I also like to understand more about what is going on in the life of the board member/investor. Push them to also provide their wins, their biggest issues, and give them feedback on what they are doing well and how they can get better.

Beyond just a call, it's also great if you can find time to meet up in person as well for lunch, dinner, or drinks. Sometimes casual conversation without an agenda can lead to open thinking where problems pop out more clearly, and solutions can become even more apparent.

CHAPTER 27

How to Run the Board Meeting

Now that you did all the board meeting preparation in the last chapter, it's time to run your meeting. The board meeting can be an incredible opportunity to get everyone together to discuss the most important topics and lay the groundwork for the major decisions of the business.

In this chapter, we will run through how to select your board meeting attendees, how to pick the agenda, and some options on how to conduct the actual meeting. We will focus on ways to ensure the meeting spends the vast majority of time focused on the top-of-mind issues for the CEO, and how to translate that to key decisions.

1. **Setting your board meeting attendee list:** Consider an expanded audience as long as it doesn't hurt your ability for transparent conversations.
2. **Making a written board culture:** Offer an environment for written feedback mixed with spoken discussion.
3. **Focusing on CEO top-of-mind:** Use the meeting to get feedback on the biggest decisions leadership needs to make at the company.

4. **Closed sessions and decisions:** Carve out sections of the meeting for smaller audiences to spend time uncovering and discussing potentially sensitive questions.
5. **Open access and information:** Consider transparency and wide communication channels across your executive team to facilitate speed and execution.

Setting Your Board Meeting Attendee List

The board meeting should include everyone the CEO wants to help make critical decisions at the company. At my businesses, I like to include all of my direct reports in board meetings. Most of them don't speak very much in the meeting, but they have the opportunity to follow the conversation in real time and provide thoughtful feedback in their areas of expertise.

By having a broader internal attendee list for board meetings, it's also a lot easier to get buy-in and understand the thinking behind major decisions. I've found that if someone doesn't attend the meeting, they can miss out on critical components of the decision process, and therefore they may not agree with or fully understand a particular decision.

Big meetings can sometimes lead to less open conversation. Someone may be afraid to say something controversial in a board setting. Two things to overcome this issue. First, I tell my team to speak openly with the board because we want to maximize their ability to help us. If you don't trust your board or if you withhold information from them, then you have bigger problems. Second, I create a closed session that includes only the board of directors. This allows time for the board to say and discuss things they may have been uncomfortable saying in the larger group because it may have hurt a relationship with an executive at the company. We will cover more on that in the "Closed Session" at the end of this section.

Making a Written Board Culture

Most board members love to talk in board meetings, but unfortunately most of what is said is quickly forgotten and endlessly repeated. By focusing on a strong written culture before and during board meetings, the CEO can maximize the value they can pull from their board.

For all board meetings, I use a confidential notes document. In the meeting itself, we balance between written feedback, and spoken feedback. I've found that if you focus too much on written feedback, you run into two issues: You find less creative problem-solving, and people have a lot less fun in the board meeting and thus are less engaged.

Focusing on CEO Top-of-Mind

Before the meeting, I populate the agenda for the meeting using the survey results from the board. As a reminder, though, the meeting exists to give advice and help to the CEO, and the CEO sets an agenda to maximize how much information they can gather. A typical meeting could look something like this:

- Wins: A quick review of the successes of the business. Important to start on a positive note and acknowledge all the stuff we are doing right (five minutes).

- Top issues from CEO top-of-mind: I remind everyone of the top CEO issue #1, and based on their feedback, I share what I think my next action will be. I may have a specific question for the group, or I may have an open-ended question. In either case, I ask everyone to write their answers in the Google Document live under a feedback section. Once people have written their answers, I then go through each board member to talk about their answer and open the door for dynamic conversation that could potentially yield more ideas and solutions (30–45 minutes per issue).
- Other topics from board survey: In collecting survey responses from the board, I often find at least one other topic that pops up and makes its way to my radar as a top of mind topic. This is important to expand the view of what issues exist, but also in showing the board the CEO's ability to listen to their perspective and give additional time to the issues the board thinks are most important. In my experience, they are often right.

Closed Sessions and Decisions

I like to keep at least an hour at the end of every board meeting for a closed session, where attendance is limited to the board only. For my closed session, I offer the first half of the session with just the board of directors, excluding any full-time employees of the company. The second half includes the board plus the CEO and any other full-time employees currently on the board of directors.

In the first closed session, the board is responsible for creating a list of what they believe will be the main actions and takeaways from the meeting. While this is happening, the CEO creates their own separate list of actions and thoughts based on the board meeting. In the second joint session, the CEO compares his/her list of actions with the board's list, and hopefully we see a lot of similarities. Where we see differences, we talk them out to determine a final outcome, which is ultimately decided by the CEO.

After the board meeting, I also like to jump on the phone and have quick phone calls one-on-one with a few of the board members. Sometimes there is additional feedback that was not shared in the closed session which can be helpful for overall company strategy and operations. I just ask them, "Is there anything else you think we missed or that you noticed in the board meeting?" I often like to follow up a week or so later with some board members, as they can have some additional thoughts and ideas after they have had a chance to think more about our problems.

Open Access and Information

I like to be extremely open with the board of directors and investors in the company in order to build trust and also maximize their ability to help me execute on the problems of the business. As a result, I also let anyone on my executive team meet directly with board members and share thoughts, questions, or updates with a board member directly when relevant.

Some CEOs and companies strictly limit access to the board, so that all communications must go through the CEO. In these cases, the CEO is often insecure and/or threatened to have their team engage with the board. In my experience, though, this behavior backfires and leads to worse outcomes.

The board will sense that the CEO is guarding access, and will end up finding a way to connect with the current or former executive leaders through another channel. The board may then learn additional information from those contacts and lose trust in the CEO of the company.

CEOs should be confident in their position, especially if they are cofounders of the business. The reality is that a CEO is extremely hard to change or replace. It's very high risk. Investors do not want to change the CEO unless things are going really bad. Embrace openness and transparency across your board and executive team, and you will find a lot more help and trust to execute on your mission.

Afterword: Do What You Want to Do

Life is short. Time goes very fast. No one else is really going to care what you do unless you solve a big problem for them. Everyone is in their own TV show where they are the main star. Your family and close friends will notice what you do, but most others will not care. This may sound a bit depressing, but I've found it provides a ton of freedom. You should have no fear of what other people think. You should pursue what you want to do with your own entrepreneurial endeavors.

Do what you want to do with your life.

I love building stuff to solve problems. I love working with people that I enjoy being around. Startups can bring both. I hope this book is helpful to you, and I wish you the best of luck.

If you have questions or need some additional advice, please feel free to email me at ProblemHunting@gmail.com or follow me on Twitter @BrianCLong.

Acknowledgments

This book would never have happened without my lifelong best friend and business partner, Andrew Jones. Andrew and I have been cofounders to both of our businesses, TapCommerce and Attentive, along with a long list of failed endeavors. Andrew is the best product visionary out there, and sees around every corner. A lot of the ideas and content of this book have come through countless working sessions together to tackle these issues at our businesses.

As I mentioned in the introduction, none of these startups mentioned in this book would be successful without the support of my colleagues. I've been lucky to have a subset of people who worked with me for well over a decade at TapCommerce and Attentive. Thanks to Eric Miao, Brooke Burdge, Ethan Lo, Ryan Tsang, Brian Malkerson, Sean Grayson, and Sean McDermott. It would never have been possible without you. I could go on for pages and pages about how much impact they all had, and how much they have each helped me, and I am so thankful we got a chance to build together.

A special thanks to Jim Payne, one of my best friends and an incredible mentor. After selling his startup to Twitter, Jim helped lead the acquisition of TapCommerce (a Herculean task). Later on, Jim was an early investor in Attentive and an extremely helpful board member. Also thanks to all of my great MoPub friends, including Nafis Jamal for all his guidance and help, Kevin Weatherman, and Natalie Sandoval.

A tremendous thanks to my executive assistant, Ashley, who has helped build Attentive from a handful of people to over a thousand employees by helping run our executive office and operations every day. Thank you—I couldn't do it without you.

Over the past several years, I've also been lucky to work with Matt Mochary, the best CEO coach in the world. Matt has helped me to develop as a leader and forge many of the concepts in the "Culture" section of the book. Thank you, Matt.

For TapCommerce, we had an incredible team, and I wish to thank all of them, especially Samir Mirza (our cofounder and CTO), Shanif Dhanani, Jessica Posey, Andrew Schneider, and Tim "Papa" Geisenheimer. For Attentive, we have an amazing team today. I want to especially thank those who helped build and sell our initial MVP Attentive product including: Elyssa Albert, Jon Cox, Anthony Santomo, Andrew Bentley, Ben Blankenmeister, and Justin Yeh. I also want to thank John Trani, our fantastic head of legal who also helped review this book.

A special thanks to Scott Friend at Bain Capital Ventures, who led the Series A in both TapCommerce and Attentive and sat on both boards. Scott has been a true mentor and partner for over a decade and helped Andrew and I tremendously at every turn.

An additional big thank-you to the three other investors who have invested in both my companies: Eniac Ventures (especially Hadley Harris and Nihal Mehta, who hired me as an intern and later sent me my first term sheet), Nextview Ventures (especially David Beisel), and IVP/RRE (especially Eric Wiesen and Tom Loverro, who was at RRE for TapCommerce and IVP for Attentive).

Thanks to Pat Grady from Sequoia Capital, who led our Series B, and who I've seen is almost always right on everything. Also thanks to Sonya Huang and Doug Leone; it wouldn't have happened without you.

Thanks to Lucas Swisher and Thomas Laffont from Coatue, who helped accelerate our business to the next level and beyond, and always has a great viewpoint on every strategic question. Thanks to Rajeev from Sapphire for his nonstop support and ideas. Thanks to Dan Sundheim and Mike Tully from D1, for providing great advice during some of the most turbulent times. Thanks to Matt Witheiler from Wellington, for lots of strategic support as we grew. Thanks to Scott Dorsey at High Alpha, who helped us learn a lot from his work building ExactTarget. Thanks to Stephen from Frontline, along with Carter and Niklas from Atomico, on helping build out our European expansion. And also a big thanks to our friends across a wide set of investment firms.

Thanks to my publisher Michael Campbell, who helped provide fantastic direction. For those considering writing a book, get publisher feedback early and it will save you a lot of time! Thanks to Susan Barnett, for editing my copy, which needed a lot of grammar help.

Finally, I want to thank some of my early managers who helped get me into the tech and startup games. Thanks to Jim Loughran at CNET, who hired me for my first job and helped train me on the basics of tech sales. Thanks to Chris, Zephrin, and Geoff, who brought me into Pontiflex, and Jeff

Gottesman, who taught me some of the love of sales, and left us too early.

While I hope some of the stories in this book will help you to build your dream business, I know you will make lifelong friends through your entrepreneurial journey. Thank you.